"SHUT UP, BITCH!"

James Evans, 15, pushed the old woman back with all his might as she tried to escape him. He grabbed her around the neck from behind, both gloved hands tightening. His anger leapt out of control, and he yanked back hard.

In the movies and on TV shows, an actor could pull back like this and the victim's neck would snap. But they had it wrong—Betty Gardner only struggled harder. This wasn't anywhere near as easy as he had thought it would be.

"Remember this, bitch," Evans snarled through his teeth. "You're never going to be able to hit Wendy again."

He squeezed tighter. The old woman had a lot of fight. Keeping his stranglehold, he fumbled for the three-foot long piece of nylon-reinforced kite string. Evans wound the kite string around her neck, pushed her down, then planted his foot on her back.

He curled the fingers of his right hand around the thin string on her neck and pulled taut.

Betty Gardner continued to struggle until she blacked out. Evans held on.

She stopped gasping for air and went limp.

BOOK YOUR PLACE ON OUR WEBSITE AND MAKE THE READING CONNECTION!

We've created a customized website just for our very special readers, where you can get the inside scoop on everything that's going on with Zebra, Pinnacle and Kensington books.

When you come online, you'll have the exciting opportunity to:

- View covers of upcoming books
- Read sample chapters
- Learn about our future publishing schedule (listed by publication month *and author*)
- Find out when your favorite authors will be visiting a city near you
- Search for and order backlist books from our online catalog
- Check out author bios and background information
- Send e-mail to your favorite authors
- Meet the Kensington staff online
- Join us in weekly chats with authors, readers and other guests
- Get writing guidelines
- AND MUCH MORE!

**Visit our website at
http://www.kensingtonbooks.com**

KILL
GRANDMA
FOR ME

Jim DeFelice

Pinnacle Books
Kensington Publishing Corp.

http://www.pinnaclebooks.com

Some names have been changed to protect the privacy of individuals connected to this story.

I

INNOCENCE ON TRIAL

Prologue

An Innocent's Innocence

Winter 1997

Another time, another place, they could have been Romeo and Juliet, two star-crossed teens bucking the gods and their families for a once-in-an-eon passion, the kind of love that stops your heart and changes your life. They fell for each other and into each other, and if this were Verona or some fairy tale, they might have turned up in a castle or at least a sonnet, mourned by the ages as models of idyllic love.

But this was the 1990s, a time when middle-class values could erode in a sound-byte minute, a time when violence French-kissed passion, and even love cloaked itself in bloody rags. And this was Saugerties, a small town in upstate New York, a place of well-measured lawns and bowling alleys, pizza joints that closed no later than nine, and strip malls haunted by lead-footed teens in rebuilt Camaros. Dreams here came not from what your father did but from what was playing at the local movie theater. Passion wasn't dead, it had just crammed itself into the dark shadows, hidden in the thump of rap music suburban white kids played as they cruised the state highway down to the shopping mall.

So when Betty Gardner tried to keep her thirteen-year-old granddaughter Wendy from seeing fifteen-year-old James Evans, a local boy with a bad reputation, the sixty-seven-year-old grandma ended up strangled to death, a nylon-reinforced kite string twisted around her neck.

It wasn't the most efficient murder ever, but it worked in its own grim fashion. For two days, James and Wendy made love and ate junk food and hit the mall and made love some more. They drove grandma's Mercury up into the Catskills and down the state highway—with grandma's body locked in the trunk the whole time. They ran through almost $800 the old lady on a fixed income had carefully stashed away for bills, spending the wad of cash on pizza, video games and sexy underwear.

When the cops finally knocked on their door New Year's Eve, neighbors and family members were stunned. Almost unanimously, they pinned the blame on James—the bratty bully everyone believed was shotgunning toward a life of petty crime and probably worse. Wendy had been a model child until she met him in the summer of 1994: quiet, well-behaved, an overachiever in school. True, her mother was a prostitute and her father an admitted substance abuser who had lost custody of Wendy and her sister ten years before. But everyone thought they knew who Wendy Gardner was—a smiling, friendly child who looked like a toy doll and whose most ambitious crime was acting like a tomboy. Until she met James, she was the very image of prepubescent innocence.

But things were never that simple.

In February 1997, more than two years after her arrest on the charge of premeditated murder, Wendy Gardner walked into Ulster County Court. She wore a demure, floor-length dress, looking all the world like a cherubic angel. Small for her age, with a round face and straight, shoulder-length hair, she was the girl next door, the daughter you hoped for, the above-average student with a flair for music and a talent for art. Her lawyer was a former New York City tough guy who'd escaped Hell's Kitchen to become one of the top defense attorneys in New York's historic Hudson River Valley. Wendy had been barely thirteen when the murder occurred. Thirteen isn't even old enough to get into the average movie at the cineplex—but it is old enough to get an adult murder rap in New York, one of the toughest states in the nation on juvenile crime.

That cold day in February, the lawyer tugged heavy on the heartstrings as he wove his line of defense in his opening statement. With careful, commonsense logic, he explained how the little girl had been held hostage by James Evans, made to go along with a crime she never wanted to happen. He had psychiatrists and other witnesses to prove it.

The jury seemed to buy it, even as the prosecution brought out the police detective who had popped the lid on a well-kept 1984 Mercury in the driveway of the house on Appletree Drive. Strangling does unkind things to people's faces; Betty Gardner's puffed up and was tinted with rose-colored bursts by the time the medical guy got there. But the jurors expected this, as gruesome as it sounded—they knew there had been a murder. The question was what had Wendy done, how culpable was she for her grandmother's death? Neither the detective nor the other cops who spoke that first morning could implicate her directly.

The jurors took turns studying the girl as the trial wore on. She seemed shell-shocked by the entire proceeding, a victim of post-traumatic stress disorder.

The assistant district attorney called a state police investigator to the stand.

A statement had been taken from Wendy on New Year's Eve, had it not?

It had.

It had been taped, in fact, had it not?

It had.

And is this the tape?

It is.

The assistant district attorney asked that the jury be allowed to hear it.

The room hushed. The jurors, watching Wendy, moved forward in their seats. Here it was, they thought, here was the explanation of what had happened, the vindication of an innocent's innocence.

The tape started to roll.

II

TRUE LOVE

1

Snapdragon

July 1994

"My peace is My gift to you, and I do not give it to you as the world gives it."

The words from the gospel echoed against the stone blocks of the church, its gothic interior lit by the rays of a powerful summer sun. Twelve-year-old Wendy Gardner sat in the thickly varnished wooden pew of Our Lady of the Snow Roman Catholic Church, listening as the priest explained the mysteries of the Trinity and the promise of everlasting life. God could seem distant and severe, but He was an important part of her life, a visceral presence as real as the thick walls of the working man's church set on the edge of a hill not far from the center of Saugerties village. Gardner's grandmother, Elizabeth, sitting next to her in the pew, studied the bible intensely and preached its virtues relentlessly to her granddaughter. She often told her friends that she strove to live her life by the Good Book; most thought she succeeded remarkably well, despite the influence of the times. Even raising her two granddaughters by herself—Wendy and Kathy, who was two years younger than Wendy—had not bent her devotion to the word of God.

If there was anyone in the half-filled church that mid-summer morning who looked the very picture of angelic devotion, it was Wendy Gardner. The gently rounded preteen had a sweet, ready smile, though at times she could seem painfully shy. The twelve-year-old had a gift for music—her flute playing had already attracted academic notice—and it would not take a particularly poetic bent for anyone spotting her to describe the not quite four-foot, ten-inch girl as a cherub, an honored member of the celestial choir surrounding God and singing his praise.

But the private world of her thoughts was anything but angelic. Having passed through puberty months before, the twelve-year-old was having a difficult time adjusting to her body's changes. At times, she felt like several different people, racked by desires and hormones she couldn't completely understand, much less control. Part of her was very much a little girl, cherishing dolls and frilly toys, and part of her was a tomboy who loved to test herself in athletic contests against the neighborhood boys. Outside of her grandmother's sight, Gardner wore an awkward veneer of sexual sophistication, and a longing so frank that neighbors warned her not to throw herself at boys. Even now, as she prayed with the rest of the congregation, she couldn't help thinking about the warmth that came from having a boy hold her and stroke her breasts.

Every day she confided some of her feelings in a small, clasp-lock diary, the kind young teenage girls have kept for generations. The cover illustration echoed her personality: a delicate rose tied in a ribbon over a piece of sheet music, which itself lay atop a brick wall. With her entries protected by a simple metal lock, Wendy told the lightly lined pages things she would volunteer to no one else.

"My life is so unpredictable," she had written when she started the diary that summer. "I don't know when I'm going to be happy or sad, disappointed or mad, if I'll be able to be in love or just in a stupid messed-up game that my boyfriends play on me."

She also had written a warning on the front cover:

> To anyone who finds this Diary, and reads it (unless given it, or asked to read it) I hope they burn in hell!

> Wendy Gardner

> p.s.
> If you won't go to Hell, I'll kill you and I will.

Few if any children reaching puberty ever feel as if they belong anywhere. Wendy Gardner had special reasons to feel different. No one else in the neighborhood was being raised by his or her grandmother, and few shared the kind of tumult that had marked Wendy's years as an infant and toddler.

While her father, Clarence "Buzz" Gardner Jr., saw her often, even he would later admit under oath that he had hardly been a consistent, positive presence in his daughters' lives. He occasionally went months without seeing either of them.

Betty Gardner had gone to court and won custody of her two granddaughters in 1987 after Buzz's life and marriage had hit what must have seemed rock bottom. It had been headed in that direction a long time. Gardner's only child, Buzz had graduated from Saugerties High School in 1968. His former lawyer described him as one of millions of kids lured by the siren song of drugs and alcohol; like many, he found his life inextricably changed by them. Over the years, he was charged with a number of petty crimes. According to his lawyer, the offenses were generally related to substance abuse. By the nineties, Buzz described himself as a subcontractor, a worker in the housing and construction industry, which ebbed and flowed with the health of the local economy. His relationship with his parents was hardly idyllic; he claimed his father was a violent ogre, and prided himself on having argued with him the day the man died.

While capable of showing great love, even on good days Buzz Gardner could be extremely volatile. He had seen his marriage to Wendy's mother Jann disintegrate into a hazy netherworld marked by their permanent estrangement and then her prostitution in nearby Poughkeepsie, a small city across the river about thirty minutes south of Saugerties. The only thing acquaintances differed about when describing her was which drugs she was addicted to.

Wendy would later tell a psychiatrist that she vaguely remembered the conflict between her father and mother that marked the end of her parents' relationship, which if true would have taken place when she was still very young. As she told it, the dispute started with a fight over a cigarette, and ended with her mother trying to stab her father. Her father later told a court-appointed psychiatrist that Jann had used heroin and cocaine even during her pregnancy with Wendy.

By the summer of 1994, Jann Gardner was living in a drug-infested, cockroach-laden area of Poughkeepsie. She had been infected with HIV sometime before, and knew she was going to die.

Wendy's early years could best be described as chaotic. Still, a family friend called her "one of my favorite toddlers of all time," stating that Wendy "was all sunshine and love and smiles" despite her parents' problems. As traumatic and difficult as her first surroundings may have been, the young girl thrived at first under her grandmother's care. Betty's husband Clarence, an Army vet and blue collar worker employed in the cement and gravel industry and active in the union, had passed on unexpectedly a few years earlier, and Wendy and Kathy were now the focus of their grandmother's attention. By all accounts, Betty Gardner was strict with the girls, so much so that she seemed out of step with the times. Her home was modestly furnished; money was always tight, and Betty had only recently begun to draw Social Security. The girls were nonetheless well-fed and clothed, and they always impressed others as being well-behaved.

But resentment toward her grandmother gurgled in Wendy's chest that summer as she approached her thirteenth birthday. The twelve-year-old could cite many slights. Her anger erupted when Betty told her she couldn't go to the mall in nearby Kingston, a fifteen or twenty-minute car ride away, because she was too young. Wendy thought it was really because the old woman couldn't stand to miss any of her beloved soap operas.

Her granddaughter called her a bitch—not to her face—and moped all day about it.

Gardner also resented her grandmother's attempts to involve her in family outings, though the occasions—like swimming in a relative's pool—generally turned out to be fun. Betty even tried to restrict Wendy from calling boys on the telephone. The old woman's disapproval was a thick fog that hung everywhere in the house. Wendy chafed under Betty Gardner's conservative ways and hid the extent of her sexual involvement with boys.

The young girl was also disturbed by her father's conflicts with her grandmother. One summer morning she woke to a fight between them when her father wanted to borrow a hundred dollars—money the older woman could not afford to lend out, and which she undoubtedly thought would never be repaid.

At least some part of Wendy Gardner's feelings toward her grandmother came from her perception—laser-accurate, according to impartial adult friends—that Betty favored Wendy's younger sister Kathy. It was Kathy who got new soccer shoes; Wendy got hand-me-downs because her feet were smaller. In a household with scarce resources, every purchase that wasn't for her could seem like a slight. Wendy did not begrudge her younger sister; she loved her to death and spent much of her time with her. But she especially hated it when her grandmother's lectures about behavior included references to Wendy's mother. To Betty, Jann was evil incarnate, and the older woman said Wendy was cut from the same dark wood.

Neighbors and others familiar with the family later said that Gardner tended to harp on Wendy's physical resemblance to her mother. She constantly told her that she would end up like her if she didn't straighten out—even though the girl committed few if any overt crimes or sins.

While Wendy greatly resented the comparisons, her attitude toward her mother, like her attitude toward practically everyone else, was complex. If she counted her father as one of her few true friends, Wendy also felt something for the woman who had left him. There was too much hate and resentment there to call it love; call it an aching hole in the heart.

The small girl with a shy smile and quiet manner did well at the Ricardi Elementary School, a two-story red brick structure tucked off the main roads about a mile from her home. The open field behind the school building readily bred daydreams, and the Hudson River rolled by within walking distance, its vast blue surface conjuring moods as variable as the waves. Still, Wendy Gardner fought off these distractions and impressed her teachers, especially in the lower grades where she got mostly B's, B+'s and A's. Diligent and hard-working, she had a creative streak that expressed itself in a number of ways. Gardner won awards for her flute performances, and could play soccer and other sports for hours. Soccer not only allowed her to express her frenetic, athletic energy in a socially acceptable way, when she did well, it would make her an accepted part of a team. She was desperate for acceptance and praise, and when she thought she would fail, she preferred to walk away rather than embarrass herself on the field. Some of the family volatility came out on the soccer field during encounters with coaches, but for the most part, Gardner made good impressions.

On report cards, teachers referred to Wendy in terms such as a "fine student who excels" and complimented her work habits. Her sixth grade year, 1993-94, was no different, and any teacher who knew her even slightly might have predicted not only a successful junior and senior high school career but a good college showing as well.

Going from elementary school to junior high school in September requires a major adjustment for teenagers. For Wendy and her classmates, the seventh grade and the rest of the junior high grades were housed in a building that also included the high school. Gardner would soon find herself dwarfed in a crowd of larger bodies. But she didn't think too much of school at any point during the summer of 1994; the closest she came to academics was reading one or two of R.L. Stine's Goosebumps series—horror stories for preteens, favored mostly by boys. She liked Stine as an author, and even contemplated writing a story in his style about the death of an ex-boyfriend.

Much of what Wendy Gardner thought about that summer concerned her ups and downs with two boyfriends, Pete Stewart and Cal Hanson. Pete was a neighbor, and he and Wendy had been going together for two years. Their relationship had survived numerous break-ups and trials and tribulations. At the tail-end of the school year, Stewart dumped her. Wendy was shocked the relationship had ended for good, not just because it was over, but because *he* had "dumped" her. In the past, she had always been the one to do the dumping, and his seeming arrogance made the slight hurt all the more. Compounding her frustration, the twelve-year-old was convinced that Pete had told his friends she was "easy." Betrayal, jealousy, and love boiled together. The volatile venom of her feelings toward him surprised even Gardner. She remained fixated on Pete even as she longed to be in Cal's arms.

Cal Hanson lived on the north side of the village, about a mile away from the Gardner house but too far for Wendy to walk. She wouldn't even ride her bike there, much as she might pine for him. He called occasionally, but they saw each other rarely. In retrospect, the relationship would seem one-sided. Wendy was constantly worried that Hanson would dump her, lamenting over long periods when he seemed to show little interest. Every so often, she would get a call from a "friend of a friend" about him, sometimes warning her that he only wanted to use her, sometimes warning her not to use him.

Writing in her diary, the young girl borrowed the crude code teenage boys often used when speaking about sex. It was based on baseball, with each station on the diamond of passion relating to a sexual achievement. "1=kiss, 2=French, 3=MO (makeout), 3 1/2=4-play, 4=Home," she wrote, in case she might forget—or perhaps because she secretly did hope someone would steal a peek and discover who she was.

According to the diary, Wendy and Pete had gone pretty far around the bases, coming close but not quite to a home run (sexual intercourse). Even so, there were obvious gaps in her sexual knowledge. While Gardner knew what a "blow job" was, she believed that a boy would "faint" if he had one.

Her needs at times were frank, perhaps even desperate. She let an old boyfriend make out with her even though she felt little if anything for him. The harshest thing she would say about a former girlfriend was "she sucks dick" all over town. A few enemies in the neighborhood now were whispering something similar about her.

Barclay Heights was an enclave of close yards and tangled cul-de-sacs, the kind of place where neighborhood kids of various ages drift in and out of friendships and alliances, an entire relationship running its course over a pickup basketball game or an afternoon in a friend's pool. To some kids, perhaps the majority, it was a secure place to grow up, a place they knew and were known. But closeness can turn claustrophobic or worse, it can persecute and ostracize rather than include. According to her diary entries, Wendy Gardner spent part of nearly every day that summer fearfully insecure, aware that she didn't fit in with the local cliques of Barclay Heights.

Bitter at slights, real and imagined, at times Wendy couldn't even take a walk without feeling humiliated by neighborhood kids. Still obsessed with Pete, she dreaded seeing him. She told her diary he "is such a fuckin' queer from hell . . . that he doesn't deserve to live or die, but I think I'll kill him so he will die . . . He torcheed [sic] me, now I'll tocher [sic] HIM. I'm going to write a threatening note, in my blood, like Death live's [sic] with you, and near you. Signed, Snap Dragon. (I say I'm gonna do a lot of things but they don't usually happen.)"

"Snap Dragon" was a reference to a movie Gardner had recently seen on television called *Snapdragon*.

Released in 1993 and rated R, the film starred Pamela Anderson as a psychotic serial killer who tricks and seduces a police psychiatrist. Anderson's character— called both Snapdragon and Felicity, representing the two different sides of her personality— is a prostitute who lures men to bed and then kills them.

Gardner seems to have seen the movie at least twice. For some days after first watching it, she tried on the personality in the safety of her imagination, but her fears and venom remained after the immediacy of the movie faded. Gardner would continue to fill the pages of her diary with them into August.

"I wonder how fun it would be to write a story about killing Pete," she mused, her hatred toward Pete Stewart growing as she sensed Cal Hanson had forgotten about her.

There were times during the summer that Wendy felt so depressed that simple things cheered her greatly. The day the optometrist told her she no longer had to wear her glasses quite as much as in the past was a high water mark. The night she stayed out until 10:15, the girl practically crowed with the accomplishment. Stretching Grandma's curfew was a major milestone, and she recorded it proudly in her diary.

Her encounters with the neighborhood kids were not all filled with disappointment and vile. Over the course of July, Gardner drew close to one girl, Brenda Gruen, relying on her as a friend, and confiding some of her secrets and dreams, though by no means the darkest.

One afternoon, the conflict with the local clique boiled over into a screaming match. Furious when one of the smaller boys called her a bitch, Wendy Gardner wanted to punch the kid, and probably would have, except for Brenda, who held her back. Wendy, in the language of the neighborhood kids, felt she could beat the shit out of the little wuss, even though he had all his friends around him. She refused to back down, cursing aloud and fuming about what she really wanted to do.

Later, she had a dream about making out with Pete. She told her diary she would rather chop him up, murder him somehow, even if it meant she would be arrested and charged with murder.

But the passion that exploded in the street had another side. Not long after the screaming fight, Wendy began considering the nature of friendship. She still divided the world into people who hated her—the vast majority—and people who loved her—an infinitesimal few. But she was beginning to see the glimmering of shadows in this black and white world, or at least the possibility that her judgments were wrong.

Earlier in the year, she had quarreled with a younger friend named Melody Winters. After Gardner had confided to Melody that she was having periods, Melody had lied and said that she was having them too. Bright and observant, Wendy immediately guessed the truth. Lying amounted to betrayal in her eyes, and the once-important friendship fell apart. But the break hurt Gardner more than Melody. Finally, as summer drew close to an end, they made up during a long and calming talk that left the twelve-year-old remarkably philosophical.

"I could tell her everything," Wendy would realize as she wrote about the friendship in her diary, "because she is a true friend, no matter what anyone else says . . . You could have a whole bunch of good friends, but only true friends stay together . . . Even if you get into really big fights . . . you find out that your friend really didn't hate you, just was upset with you about a certain situation. Your TRUE friends most of the time get into fights with you when they're trying to help you!!!!

"Remember that," she told her diary, adding, "I learned a few lessons today. One was don't let your feelings hurt another person, always resolve fights, don't hold grudges. . . . These lessons can help anyone in their life. Believe me, I know. I'm on the verge of trying it out myself."

Depending on which of Wendy Gardner's friends got together that summer, Wendy was seen as an atom bomb looking for Hiroshima or as a budding Juliet looking for Romeo—or just as an ordinary young teenager, mixed up, unsure of herself, scared to death of the world and ready to beat the crap out of it to come out on top.

She was all future, energy, and potential smashing head-on with the present. She might get swallowed up in school—or graduate at the head of the class. She might become a musician—or a seductive serial killer. Anything, it seemed, was possible.

And then she met James Evans.

2

The Bully of Barclay Heights

Scenes from the Summer 1994

James Evans' sister Donna was driving her ambulance down Route 9W one day in early 1994 as she and another attendant took a patient to the hospital. Suddenly, across the road she saw an oversized kid on a BMX bicycle cresting the hill. Disbelief turned to anger as she realized it was her younger brother James. He had run away from a home for troubled youth across the river.

It wasn't the first time.

She thought about hitting the brakes and going after him. Instead, she turned to watch in the rearview mirror as James stopped and waved from the crest of the hill. She could almost hear him laughing.

*   *   *

The strapping fifteen-year-old had a history of running away from places he didn't want to be. Voluntarily committed to the group home by his mother the year before, James had been sent there, at least partly, because he was too much for the single mother to handle. In theory, the group home, a community-based facility that from the outside looked just like any of the other middle-class houses in its suburban neighborhood, was supposed to surround him and its half-dozen or so other charges with counseling and good influences. In reality, it became for Evans a finishing school in juvenile delinquency.

When his mother visited him a few weeks before he ran away, she noticed he was wearing new sneakers.

"Where did you get those?" she asked.

"At Bob's," he answered, me referring to a local clothing store.

"Where did you get the money?"

"We all just walked in and took them," he explained, with an expression that said his mother had just asked the stupidest question in the world.

According to Evans, a group of kids from the home would routinely walk into the store in the nearby South Hills Mall, go to the back aisles where the shoes were displayed, and start trying some on. Eventually, they would find an opportunity to leave, walking out in the new sneakers, their old ones in the boxes on the shelves.

In the stories that he told his mother, Evans was always the follower, not the doer. Nonetheless, the staff at the group home considered him an accomplished troublemaker in his own right. By the time summer loomed and James went AWOL, they had had more than their fill. He'd gotten into at least one serious fight at the group home. Records indicate he had apparently stabbed one of the other boys with a hemostat, a blunt instrument ordinarily used for stopping bleeding. After a disagreement with a counselor, he took his anger out on her car, smashing it with a baseball bat. That incident resulted in family court charges. Evans was placed on probation, though ultimately the family court system, with its stronger emphasis on counseling rather than punishment, did not seem to have much of an impact on his behavior.

By the summer of 1994, Evans was a seasoned veteran of family court. He was first introduced to the court system around age eight—not as a juvenile delinquent, but as the subject of a wrenching, convoluted battle for custody between his mother and father.

Born in Kingston in 1979, the young James was a bright, cheerful boy despite his parents' violent relationship. His father would be described in court as beating his mother during the few years they were together. By the time James was two, their relationship had ended. Dinah Evans was in and out of trouble with the law and was separated from her son when he was young. She admitted later that she had spent a few months in jail (but never state prison) on minor charges when James was young. She was also well-known to the local police and the Saugerties town judge, who later recalled placing her on probation for a minor offense.

Despite the chaotic influences of his early years, James Evans' grades were good, and the family photo album shows a smiling, active kid, normal in all respects. Then one year, the smiles changed to sullen frowns, and it seemed obvious to anyone who knew him that something inside the bright little boy had broken, and broken bad.

Dinah blamed it on the custody battle. She was stunned in 1987 when the family court awarded custody of the eight-year-old to his father. Awarding custody to a father is unusual in New York State. The court cited his mother's "pathology," and her trouble with the law may have played a part in the decision. But for some reason never clearly explained, although a psychiatrist's report and some people familiar with the case speculate that James's father expected to lose an appeal, he didn't take custody of his son for several years.

That was fine with James, who reacted to the custody fight with confusion and bitter resistance. When his father finally did take custody, James physically resisted. He threatened to run away and told his mother and sister that he didn't want to leave the people who loved him.

Finally in 1990, the eleven-year-old Evans was ordered to live with his father in a rural upstate community more than a hundred miles away from the only home he had ever known. James tried running away several times, and had to be wrestled by his older and much larger brother before he would agree to go.

A neighbor familiar with the family described the father as a decent, hard-working man, but whether it was because of the discipline his dad tried to impose, the fact that he hadn't grown up with him, or a myriad of other reasons, James Evans hated the idea of living with his father.

Shuffled between different school districts, his grades began a downward spiral. His teachers complained he was underachieving. Though Evans' schoolwork seemed to improve for a while, an official there thought of the young man as someone who had a poor attitude and stayed away from school.

But all was not desolate. James spent at least some of his days with his grandmother. Confined to a wheelchair, she seemed glad for his company and doted on him, making special foods for him and in general showing an uncritical acceptance he rarely found anywhere else. Meanwhile, his relationship with his father remained rocky at best.

One of his friends later described an incident during which James mourned the loss of an acquaintance killed in a bicycle accident by fantasizing that the boy would return from the dead and kill them all. The acquaintance's death gained symbolic significance for James, who recounted it for a psychiatrist as if the young man was a close friend killed en route to see him. The only people who seemed to take a genuine interest in him, he told the therapist, all died. He felt he would, too.

Evans' determination not to live with his father eventually brought him back to Saugerties. The tangled custody battle had led to his return to his mother and his voluntary placement in the group home. At the time, it seemed like a good compromise solution to a difficult and protracted tangle for custody that was doing no one, James especially, any good.

A psychologist who examined him when he was admitted to the group home noted that while on the surface James was yet "another boy with a conduct disorder," underneath "he was clearly depressed . . . sad, tired, frequently could cry." James felt his life was awful. According to the therapist, and just about everyone in the family, he had developed a front of cold-eyed stoicism, a world-weary cynicism at age fourteen.

Worse, he flashed a red-hot anger at anyone or any-thing that crossed him.

The psychologist believed that Evans needed more structure than the group home would provide. But there was no alternative. He rebelled practically from the start.

The counselors at the group home finally decided to release him back to his mother's custody in June 1994, a few weeks before the end of the 1993-94 school session. Years later, the case would still haunt them, even as they said there was nothing else they could have done to help the embittered young boy.

On the other hand, Evans had not been thrown out on the street. His mother's house on Rose Lane in the Barclay Heights section of Saugerties was a small but comfortable raised ranch, crowded with knickknacks. Shared with two dogs and an army of cats, it bore witness to Dinah's uneven domestic abilities. Homey touches like a well-cultivated pocket garden in the front yard contrasted with a car in perpetual disrepair sitting a few feet away. James' bedroom, with its Marlboro posters and boxing photos, stuffed animals and family snapshots, had plenty of room for a favorite basketball and an upholstered chair.

The strapping fifteen-year-old with a nascent mustache, shortish hair, and acne was driven to school across the river every day by his mother. His sister, about a dozen years older than he, made a special effort to be there for him, and even considered having him live with her own small family. Brother and sister clashed often. Donna had a fiercely developed sense of right and wrong, and wanted James to live up to those standards, but she loved him deeply, and James seemed to respect her as much, if not more, than he respected anyone.

Counselors met with him regularly at his home, trying to help. As the summer melted toward fall, the system tried to make up for years of neglect, paying attention to the young man with the volatile temper and hard-ass attitude.

But Dinah Evans saw her son slipping away. She blamed herself for letting him go into the group home, believing it had only made James worse. Many in the community found her unstable and volatile. She was criticized for being a less than consistent mother and a less than ideal citizen. Still, she wanted to do the right thing, and no matter what else, her love for her children never wavered. Embittered by her custody fight, she railed at the family court system which didn't want to hear about the abuse she claimed her children and she had suffered. Dinah Evans grew enraged when neighborhood kids called James a bully, believing that the stories were distortions told to make the teller look good. No angel herself, she nonetheless worried about trying to somehow save her youngest son from the path he seemed headed toward.

Just how bad James Evans really was would eventually become a matter of intense debate. Certainly after the murder of Betty Gardner it would be difficult if not impossible to find anyone in the neighborhood—outside of his immediate family—who thought he was anything but a bully and worse. By then his evil had assumed nearly mythic proportions. Evans had become the stuff suburban legends are made from, a kid who roasts kittens in microwaves and squirts pepper spray at little girls. James and his family vehemently denied those stories, which circulated in several versions through the neighborhood and found their way into a local newspaper story.

But in the summer of 1994, James Evans still had a good side, even if he showed it less and less. Spurting toward six feet and beyond, he was avoided by many for a variety of reasons, not least of which was his unpredictable and cruel temper. But the teenager at least occasionally played the role of protector, not bully, in the neighborhood. A psychiatrist would later say that Evans longed to be not a bully but a hero, and clumsily confused the roles.

There were a few bright moments as the dog days of summer lingered. One of the best came during a monster truck rally in Connecticut. It was one of the last mother-son things the once inseparable pair of Dinah and James did. That long summer night, Dinah thought to herself that the old James had returned. He even posed for a picture with some of the drivers, clearly excited and having a good time. For one glorious evening, Dinah Evans reveled in the fact that she had her son back. Nothing else—not the past, not the future, not his troubles with the law, not her troubles with the law—seemed to matter.

But it was only one brief exception in a long stretch of hot summer days. With considerable help from her daughter and older son, Dinah would never, ever give up on James. But the struggle dragged on, harder and harder, as the weather turned.

The little boy was still inside somewhere, still longing for love, still hoping to be taken seriously. But by now he had grown to inhabit an adult's body. That body let James Evans do more things; his anger became more damaging, or at least fearful to others, and he could make his will become fact. If he couldn't make everyone his friend, he could at least gain attention and some measure of fear. If his history of defiance in the court system had taught him anything, it was that adults would eventually tire of fighting him, and let him go his own way.

These were wrong and dangerous lessons to learn, though he didn't yet know that.

James Evans and his mother lived within sight of the house where Wendy Gardner lived. All of the children in the neighborhood played or hung out together at one point or another. Though they had been separated by several grades and circumstances, James and Wendy knew each other, at least vaguely, as the summer began. They moved in different circles, but had several things in common, including the absence of a strong, consistent male father figure in their lives. They were on the outside fringes of the local cliques, though such things changed like the breeze that blew across the lawns.

Older than Wendy, James never noticed her in a sexual way until sometime late that summer. Trying to fix the date for a reporter months later, James described a kid's game of tag, a laughing, teasing game where some spark passed between them, a piece of electricity that went straight to his soul, a jolt of nothing less than Destiny, sealing their two lives together in a fate neither they nor their worst enemies would ever have imagined.

3

The kiss

October 3, 1994

The first kiss was a uranium bullet to their souls, shattering the armor of their skins.

James Evans and Wendy Gardner began hanging out together sometime after Woodstock II, the massive 25th anniversary celebration of the Love and Peace generation, held on a field in the rural hillside of their hometown. There were games of tag in the neighborhood, pickup games of hoops, bicycle rides, and soccer practices. No formal dates, just encounters that began to drip with meaning and hormones.

At first, the attraction was real iffy. There were so many differences between them: Evans was tall, Gardner was short; he was fifteen, she was not yet thirteen. They presented different walls to the world: hers tended to be quiet and withdrawn, his angry and violent. In some ways, Evans with his temper and lean good looks may have reminded Gardner of her father, but then that might be said of any woman, any time. She wanted love, and was attracted by power and mystery. James seemed to have both.

Evans wanted sex. Few fifteen-year-olds in a country where even beer commercials feature bikini-clad models don't. But more than that, he wanted acceptance and love. They had needles for each other's hooks. One fall day after school they put them together.

James loomed over her, all arms and legs, all action, a willful moving forward. Wendy lay back, less obviously aggressive, perhaps a little awed. But energy flowed as their mouths intersected, and when the two young bodies fell into each other, their insides exploded with got-to-have-it-all passion. From the moment of their first kiss there was no question but they would make love. From the first second of penetration there was no question but that they would be in love forever.

4

"I want to fuck you"

Scenes from November, 1994

The dull tile of the classroom floor reflected the sullen overhead fluorescent, a grayish yellow light that cast everything bland and boring, the perfect setting for the endless drone of the teacher, whose head bobbed inanely before the scrawling scribble on the blackboard. Outside, the cool crisp air hinted that winter was on the way, even though the leaves on the stately maples that lined the nearby village streets were still clinging to the trees, crimson fireballs hovering over the dark, shaded ground.

Wendy Gardner, just turned thirteen, hunkered over her desk, so bored she might not even have known which class she was in. The teacher's voice was drowned out by the music playing in her head. "Comforter," a pop rhythm and blues tune by a group called Shai, had recently become one of her favorite songs. The song wove a fantasy of a special friend who might become a lover, a boy who knew a girl better than she knew herself, someone who could rescue her from oblivion, making everything all right just by comforting her.

In the past few weeks, Wendy had found that boy, and more, in James Evans. As the teacher continued to drone on, she took out a piece of paper and began writing him a note.

Jame$:

What's up? How's it hanging? I don't want to stay after today but I have to make up classes! If I don't I'll fail home ec and next year I do not want to even look at Mrs. B's face. She's a bitch. Almost as bad as my grandmother. No way—nobody can be that bad.

I want to fuck you and touch you and suck your dick. I want us to make love until we drop! We're going to do it even harder than last night. And I want to do it with you in the shower. That would be so cool. I hate going to school because I keep thinking of what we could be doing now if we weren't in school. Like: I could suck your dick, you could eat me out, you could suck my tits, then we could do it real slow. We'll gradually get faster and faster until I have so many orgasms I scream and you get so horny that you jizz all over me.

Talk about food for thought.

I love you!

I want you!

Wendy G.

Horny Bitch.

Evans' and Gardner's relationship had progressed rapidly from the childish games they'd played together as summer ended. Emotion and passion exploded inside Wendy in ways she had only dreamed about until now. Her fantasies of the summer were run over by the realities of the fall. What she had seen on television and in the movies paled in the endless moment of the real. Scared, thrilled, guilt-stricken, liberated—the jumble crashed inside her, exploding in marathon love romps whenever the two teens could get together. The feel of his hands over her budding breasts as they moved down her belly to her legs sent her into spasms of ecstasy; making love was a bolt of fevered passion that could break her in two.

But there was more to it than just physical sex.

The song "Comforter" came from an album entitled . . . *if I ever fall in love*. As important as sex is to the music, as important as it was to Wendy and James, the dream of romance and the joining not just of bodies but souls is even more critical. It weaves throughout the album, and wove now through Wendy's thoughts. She had found her comforter, her protector, in James, and she wanted it to go on forever, just like in the movies. She would do anything to get it to go on forever.

The teacher shot Wendy a dirty look, and she prayed the hag would think that her scribbling was related to class. There was no getting out of detention this afternoon, even if it would keep her from seeing her lover. Gardner had already forged notes from her grandmother getting her out of classes, but it was a trick she couldn't use too often, or the old bastards who ran the school would catch on.

Wendy Gardner had discovered something these past two months that she never would have predicted. Getting into trouble at school or in the neighborhood, not attending classes or paying attention, staying out late, stealing a neighbor's pears and throwing them at her house—all were another kind of aphrodisiac. Trouble made her feel important; risk made her feel alive. All her life she'd gone along with what adults wanted, even as resentment boiled inside her. Now she had found another solution: tell them to go to hell, and they couldn't do shit.

A few weeks back, James told her he had stolen some candy and sold it for money. The idea itself excited her, and she wrote a note praising him for the daring and for getting the cash. Brought up in a home where money was tight, the teenager was suddenly aware of it like never before. Gardner's doodles turned into dollar signs.

Some of her friends didn't believe Wendy Gardner was really having sex. A few thought it was just exaggerated bragging. For others, talking about sex was part of an intricate game of boast and put-down, a common adolescent ritual.

When Wendy's friend Penny saw that Wendy was working on a note to James that afternoon, she slipped a piece of paper across to her. "He's hot," Penny wrote, referring to James.

Gardner smiled. "He's mine, butt slammer," she wrote back.

"Hey James, I don't believe that you and Wendy did the horizontal mumbo," Penny answered on the paper, holding back a giggle as she pretended the note would actually go to James. "You have to prove it to me."

"At least I get some, bitch!"

"Wendy is a cum guzzling gutter slut!"

"Stupid hoe [sic] sucking pimp eating priss who doesn't know her ass from her elbow," responded Wendy. By now the seventh grader's anger had taken over, and the one-liners were replaced by a page-filling rant. The exchange was no longer a game, friendly or otherwise. "Bitch. You're a slut who fucks so many people that you can fit an elephant's dick in your fucking pussy and you smell like rotting fish that you eat every day . . . fuck you, you uppity bitch," she wrote in a frenzy.

Gardner was being criticized not just by school friends but others in the neighborhood and relatives who didn't approve of her seeing Evans. Almost none of the adults who knew them thought the relationship was healthy. Many believed James was trouble. One or two had called the police about him for various incidents they would later call bullying or mischief-making. They said later they couldn't understand the attraction—a tiny thirteen-year-old hanging around with a bruising fifteen-year-old? A quiet, studious girl walking hand-in-hand with a dropout-to-be?

Anyone looking for proof about how bad an influence Evans was on Gardner would have found it in her fall report card. For the girl who had shone in elementary school had suddenly become a C student at best, and her grades were only the proverbial tip of the iceberg.

Her marks for the first quarter, roughly the first ten weeks of the school year, when she missed at least a fifth of the classes, ranged from 50 to 95. Out of her eight classes, two teachers gave her failing grades; her science teacher made special efforts to notify Betty Gardner that things were not going well early on. But his concern was atypical. In health class, where state policy required a high absentee level result in a student's automatic failure, Gardner received an 85 at the end of the first semester. Only in December, when school records revealed she hadn't bothered to show up for weeks on end, did the district get around to notifying her that she would have to repeat health class.

Some of the teachers' remarks on her fall report card would prove darkly ironic. In English, Wendy was said to be performing "above average" even though she was given a 78. In Social Studies, where she had skipped about two weeks worth of classes, she was called "a pleasure to have in class."

Approximately 550 students went to the junior high, which was attached to the senior high school in one sprawling compound set amid acres and acres of athletic fields not far from the center of town. Close to 1500 students attended classes in the complex, a collection of sprawling rectangles in bland brown brick and painted concrete. In size alone, the school was a sharp contrast to the small elementary school Gardner had graduated from a few months before.

In her early grades, Wendy had won her teachers over with her hard work and quiet ways; in high school, she was often at odds with them. As the semester went on, Wendy Gardner simply stayed away more and more. Exactly how much time she missed would later be unclear, because the individual class records don't add up and Gardner sometimes forged notes to excuse her absences.

The thirteen-year-old with a cherubic face didn't fall entirely between the cracks. School records show that an administrator spoke to her grandmother at least once about the absences, and a few of her teachers assigned her detention. However, some of the school's actions, such as threatening a girl who was purposely missing class with suspension, made little sense. Betty Gardner complained bitterly to friends that the school was not helping her with Wendy. If there was a comprehensive plan to help the once above-average student who was now failing, it wasn't recorded in the records that would later be turned over to the county court. More importantly, it didn't work.

No matter what happened at school or what else was going on, Wendy Gardner usually found her way over to James Evans' house eventually. It was as if a magnet pulled her there, and the magnet was James.

In Wendy's mind, her grandmother didn't have a clue what love was; she thought it was something evil, and kept talking about putting an end to it. "Grams" hated James. She even told her he was "too perfect." Maybe, Wendy thought, her grandmother was jealous that she couldn't be loved the way Wendy was. Their affair was hot. It was consuming and had an edge of danger and lurking violence.

There were times when Gardner didn't like the sex. Evans could be too demanding, pushing her to make love when she didn't want to. But there was no question about the attention. There was no question about the love that oozed between them.

When her period didn't come when it was supposed to, Wendy panicked. She'd never been late like this before—but then, she'd never had sex like this before.

"If I am preg—, I want you to punch me (again) as hard as you can!!!" she wrote James.

It turned out she wasn't pregnant. And that made her love him all the more.

As evening fell one early fall day, Dinah Evans suddenly heard a shout from the other end of her house. She ran out into the hallway to find her son James holding an immense knife in one hand and Wendy Gardner in the other.

"Take this, Mom, take it," he demanded, holding the knife out to her.

Shaking a little, Dinah grabbed the long blade, then wrapped it in a thick piece of paper as her son explained that Wendy had threatened to kill herself. It was unclear why. The two had been talking about breaking up, but that didn't seem to be the whole story.

There was a small trickle of blood near the hilt of the blade. Any wounds Wendy had were minor, but no one—not Dinah, not James, not Wendy—felt relief, even as Wendy promised she would never hurt herself again.

Repeated self-mutilation, sometimes referred to as "cutting", can be a symptom of a serious psychiatric disorder, or a disorder unto itself. Still not fully understood, those suffering the disorder obtain temporary relief from emotional anguish by punishing themselves with pain. Episodes of slicing with knives, razors, and pieces of glass are typical; the arms and legs are generally the targets.

The disorder is thought to stem from troubled family situations; victims in advanced stages are often young women around Gardner's age who have been taught to direct their rage and anger inwardly by abusive or excessively repressive or restrictive parents. Physical as well as emotional abuse is often, though not necessarily, present. Episodes of self-mutilation generally begin in the early teens, and follow stressful incidents. The disorder has only recently begun to gain serious professional as well as public notice.

The Evans family was not aware of the specifics of the disorder and later described several incidents that seem to have amounted to cutting binges. Both counselor's report at the time and a psychiatrist's report later, focusing on Evans and dealing with Gardner only tangentially, also have references to Gardner's cutting incidents.

Whatever the significance of the episodes, whether they were isolated coincidences, overt cries for help, or part of a mental disorder, Wendy was apparently never examined or treated by mental health professionals for self-mutilation or related maladies.

Though she liked the girl, Dinah Evans didn't entirely approve of the affair between Wendy Gardner and her son. The incident with the knife was just the most graphic episode of how unhealthy, how obsessive the relationship was. The kids were inseparable to the point of going to the bathroom together. But she felt impotent to stop it. One day the police came to her door, demanding that she return the girl to her grandmother. Dinah told them she wasn't keeping her there, and in fact had told her to go home.

Dinah didn't like the kids making love in her house, and told her son that, but James wouldn't listen. She would admit later that she hadn't been the best discipli-

narian, but her comments made it clear that some part
of her admired the starry-eyed nature of the romance.
She was also afraid she would lose her son completely
if she pushed too hard.

Dinah Evans knew that a lot, maybe most, of her
neighbors looked down on her and her crowded yard
and home. To them, she was nothing but a worthless,
dysfunctional mother with a lot of cats. To them, the
fact that she rescued the neighborhood strays and gave
them a home was a sign of bad character, not kindness.
It felt galling, but there was little she could do.

Counselors were seeing James on a regular basis, and
Dinah urged Wendy to talk to them as well. But the
more people tried to tell them to "chill," the closer
the two teens became. The house seemed to vibrate
with their sex, and the best Dinah managed was to tell
them to use "protection."

She invited Wendy to spend the Thanksgiving Day
holiday with her family. Dinah could tell the girl genuinely liked her, and was looking forward to spending
the time as part of a family.

Late one night in November, James Evans sat in his
chair and reread another of Wendy's letters, one that
she had composed several days before.

>   James,
>   I love you SO much. It wasn't your fault. All the
>   stuff that happened, happened. It was mostly all
>   my fault!!! I was being so fucking stupid. Do you
>   think I should go to a psychologist or a coun-
>   selor??? It might help me out a little.
>   Those past two nights were WAY too perfect.

But I'm really glad they happened, only because of you. If you weren't there, it would've been SO HARD FOR ME!!! When I started crying (on the bus) you were right there to help me. I am confused. Now the stuff that happened feels like it didn't happen at all . . .

I can't believe my grandma tried to con me into dumping you! When I got home this morning I tried lying to her, but that didn't work. So I had to tell her the truth. I couldn't hold it in any longer. Thank God I didn't cry!!! I snapped on the bus because so many things [are] going on in my head! It sucked . . .

This might sound stupid, but you should tell your mom you skipped so in case she does find out, she won't "kill" you. Plus and if you tell her, she'll consider you to be an honest person and you can get away with it . . .

Wendy had left his room long ago, sneaking back to her house and bed as she usually did. Evans, sitting in his darkened bedroom, carefully tucked the letter into the folder where he saved the others.

Though he rarely if ever answered her letters, he valued them immensely. They were genuine proof of the greatest thing that had ever happened to him. Just a few months before he had been lonely and unloved, worthless. Now he found himself at ground zero of a love tornado.

It was great, but it was a hell of a ride. There were downs as well as huge highs. At times, Wendy acted like she wanted to break things off; at other times, she seemed willing to climb inside his chest if she could.

And then there was all the drama with the knives. One time she even held one to his neck.

But somehow it only made him love her more.

The group home Evans had gone to the year before was in a district across the river. New to the junior-senior high, he cultivated a tough-guy image. He would stand up to anybody, and didn't mind getting into a fight, at least not that he would ever admit. James knew he was far from stupid, but he didn't put in anything like the effort that might have showcased his abilities. School, in his opinion, wasn't worth it. Teachers and principals and most other adults for that matter were jerks.

But not Wendy. Wendy was way different. No one, not even his mother or sister, loved him the way she did. And it wasn't just the sex.

James Evans had his own soundtrack playing in his head, every bit as starry-eyed sappy-romantic as Wendy Gardner's. One night after a minor argument when Wendy claimed she was going to break up with him, James dropped to his knees and began singing the Boys II Men song, "On Bended Knee." Like the singer in the song, Wendy gave him a new life; just as Wendy did, he dreamed and fantasized about spending the rest of his days with her.

Their relationship was complicated, however. One day Wendy told him about her old boyfriend, Pete, claiming that he was going to do bad things to her. Evans' anger welled up and he told her he would beat the kid up. Gardner grabbed him and begged him not to do anything.

Evans realized that she had somehow been using him, stoking him up maybe, as if it were a test. Still, it didn't change his deep urge to protect her, to do anything he had to to keep her from being hurt. If he consciously made himself out to be a bad-ass most of the time, he also had a genuinely protective side, a part that wanted to keep girls and women from being hit, even if his own anger might flash at them. He didn't see either role as contradictory; he didn't really see them as roles at all. All he saw was love and the endless possibilities of life.

If people just let him do what he wanted to do.

5

"Go back to bed"

Early December

The noise came out of nowhere, a bang in the middle of the night that reminded Betty Gardner of the days her husband walked down the hallway to the bathroom, sending her mind back more than a decade, back before the girls came to live with her, back even before the trouble with her son Buzz began. For a brief second, for the barest moment in the dark of the small bedroom, Betty didn't know where she was, or what had made the sound. But she responded as she always responded— not by cowering beneath the covers, not by shrinking back in the dark, but by confronting her fears, getting up and calling out to see who was there. She was just fumbling for her glasses when the answer came back.

"Just me getting water, Gram."

It was Wendy.

The girl had become an almost unbearable handful over the past few months. For the most part, Betty blamed James Evans, but she knew it was more than that. She feared that the blood of Wendy's mother ran too strongly in the girl's veins—you couldn't look at Wendy and not see Jann, the hooker. No matter how often Betty warned her, Wendy would not listen. Her grades were heading toward the gutter, and her mouth ran something awful.

Before going to bed, Betty Gardner had prayed to God not just for Wendy, but for help in dealing with her. Betty Gardner prayed a great deal, and none of her prayers were more important to her than those for her granddaughter. She had devoted a considerable portion of her life to Wendy and her sister Kathy; from attending their soccer games to hand-washing their clothes to painting their bedroom herself, much of her life revolved around them and their needs, not her own.

Betty's mind drifted back to a conversation she had had a few weeks before with the local police chief, Gregory Hulbert. She had called him many times. Generally, she didn't get through, but this day she had. She recognized the affable, almost apologetic voice on the other end, let him wade through the small talk for a few seconds, then cut to the bone.

"If these kids are in my bedroom," she said, leaving out the obvious details because they were too painful to speak, even to a policeman, "What can I do?"

Chief Hulbert hemmed and hawed. They'd been over this before. While his men had been to the house and knew the Evans kid well enough to know he wasn't exactly a saint, teenagers shacking up wasn't exactly a capital offense. Finally he told her that James could be arrested for trespassing.

"But then my granddaughter will blame me," said Gardner. "Can't *you* do anything?"

She listened to the excuses for a while longer before hanging up, exasperated. In her opinion, the town police were impotent. The state police had helped her, but even they could only do so much. There was no enforcing right and wrong any more.

In the old days, in the days when her husband was alive, when they were first married, way back during the second World War—that was when people still believed in something. That was when people still feared God. A sin was a sin.

It was still a sin. But she didn't know how to get it all through that thick head of Wendy's, the thick head she'd inherited from Jann.

Wendy must have inherited it from Jann, not from her son. She was a girl.

"Gram?" asked Wendy.

"What are you doing?"

"Nothing. Just getting water, like I said."

Betty Gardner had a vague notion that, far from having gotten up to get water, Wendy was just getting home. Had she snuck over to that Evans' house again, over to the no-good boy with the no-account mother? Had she fallen asleep in some neighbor's yard, as she had some nights before?

It would be the scandal of the neighborhood, and worse.

Betty Gardner hated to be talked about, hated to be pointed at. She tried her best and had worked hard all her life. She'd gone through the Depression as a child, and she knew the value of hard work.

Her husband had, too, God rest his soul. He lay six feet deep a few thousand yards up the road in the church cemetery. Taken from her in his prime, God rest his eternal soul.

"Go back to bed," she muttered. She slipped back beneath the covers herself.

As she drifted back to sleep, she heard her granddaughter's feet gently pad back toward her room.

Did she hear giggling, too? Or was it an angel whispering in her ear, telling her to rest now?

Betty's husband Clarence Gardner was one of the hundreds of thousands of veterans who served their country in World War II and immediately afterwards. An MP, he put in hitches in Germany and Korea; by 1951, Betty and Clarence were living in Kingston, where Betty had been born. Like much of postwar America, the city was undergoing a period of prosperity and great change. A relatively unknown company called IBM was developing machines that would revolutionize business. Before long the area between Poughkeepsie and Kingston would swell with IBMers, and the Hudson Valley would become the de facto capital of mainframe computing. The population surged, houses and shopping malls springing up in old corn fields and apple orchards throughout Ulster and neighboring counties. The Barclay Heights subdivision in Saugerties where Betty and Clarence went to live was part of that general boom.

At the same time, older industries were dying. Saugerties, the largest town in Ulster County, had been an industrial powerhouse in the nineteenth century, thanks partly to the rushing creek that lies in the middle of town, and partly to the work ethic of the Irish and other European immigrants who helped fill the factories powered by it. Much of that early development had been jump-started by one man, Henry Barclay, an industrialist and idealist who tried to impose his vision of utopia on the rough and tumble land in the heady days of capitalism before the Civil War. He made iron and paper, imported workers, established housing for them, gave money to start churches and thought of every person in town, many of whom were his employees, as family. But the industrious idealist was an easy mark for dreamers and schemers. He died separated from most of his once-vast fortune.

History responded with that special treatment reserved for visionaries flattened by reality: it forgot him. By the time the subdivision just south of the village adopted his name, few residents could say exactly what Barclay had done, beyond owning a large piece of property with a good view of the countryside.

Clarence Gardner, like his son, got the nickname "Buz" or "Buzz". He worked in a local cement plant and as an operating engineer (a heavy equipment engineer) for one of the quarries in the area. Described by some old-timers who knew him as a "decent fellow," he was active in his union, serving for a while as a business agent. His death in 1983, at age fifty-four, shocked Betty, filling her with a deep grief. Like so many Irish-American Catholics, she sought refuge in the church. Her experience led her to establish a support group for other widows. Besides going to mass and other parish activities, she devoted considerable time to the group. Her big, silver-gray 1984 Mercury, its dark navy landau top resplendent despite the car's age, could often be found parked in the church parking lot in the middle of town.

*   *   *

Wendy Gardner lied that night to her grandmother about getting water. She had actually just come home, as she bragged to James the next day. The old woman had gotten "played". Fooling Betty made her granddaughter feel good.

The relationship between grandmother and granddaughter, uneasy during the summer, deteriorated rapidly as the fall days grew cold. Emboldened by her love affair and taking cues from James, Wendy embraced the role of teenage rebel, even though she was barely a teen. She was starting to drink wine coolers like James did and spent as much time as possible hanging out with her boyfriend.

Gardner found a new way to defy her grandmother, one that hurt the deeply religious older woman: she decided she would not make confirmation.

For a Roman Catholic, the sacrament of confirmation is a milestone event. Believers enter into the faith with baptism, but in most instances that takes place when they are infants. Presented by their parents and family, they are passive participants, with little choice in the matter. At confirmation, generally celebrated as an early teen, a Catholic renews his or her faith in the presence of a bishop. The vow to renounce Satan and sin, first voiced at baptism, is renewed as a central part of the ceremony. It is an important sacrament and milestone, even in families that are only semi-devout.

When Wendy told her grandmother and the rest of her family before Thanksgiving that she wasn't going to study for confirmation, Betty felt it was a personal affront, and more. Her worst fears of Wendy turning out like her mother seemed to be coming true. She could do nothing about the girl's behavior. Wendy's schoolwork had crashed. Every time the phone rang, Betty feared it would bring some new complaint. She had tried everything she could think of to get Wendy away from James Evans, even calling his mother and arguing for hours with her, though she detested the woman.

For Wendy, dumping confirmation had a practical as well as symbolic value, since not attending the classes would give her more time to spend with James and more time making love, the only thing she wanted to do.

The way Wendy told it, hurting her grandmother was only fair. Her grandmother had been hurting her for a long, long while.

For months and even years, neighbors later said, they had heard shouts and screams coming from the house on Appletree Drive. There were different opinions about them. Some thought the grandmother went too far trying to discipline the children. A neighborhood girl told her mother and later a newspaper reporter a story of Betty Gardner grabbing Wendy by the breast and dragging her inside because she had lost a sewing needle in the grass. Some blamed the yelling on a clash of generations. Maybe Gardner's methods weren't "politically correct," but she was doing the best she could with a difficult situation. James Evans was a bad influence, and the girl's father was even worse. Screaming fights with him over money erupted on a semi-regular basis, and it wasn't much of a secret that he had done drugs and generally made a mess of his life.

Wendy first told Dinah Evans that her grandmother was abusing her after Dinah tried to get the girl to go back home one day in early fall. The incidents had enough details to make them sound convincing: having her head cracked in a bathtub for taking a bath, being pushed down stairs. To Dinah, the girl clearly seemed frightened of her grandmother.

At least one counselor who was seeing James Evans filed a complaint with Child Protective Services about the abuse allegations. There are references to it in court papers used to prepare a psychiatric evaluation. The investigation seems to have been started no later than December 1, 1994. But there is no indication that the investigation was completed, and a subpoena of the Department of Social Services, the parent agency of CPS, failed to turn up a record of that or any other investigation. No direct documentation of the charges or their disposition was ever located by anyone, or introduced in court.

When queried about the accusations of abuse, a spokesman for the department told a local newspaper tartly that all allegations were promptly investigated and that if no action was taken, that spoke for itself—if the girl had remained in the grandmother's custody, then there must not have been a basis for any allegation.

He cited confidentiality laws in avoiding any other comment or answering any other question.

One late fall day Wendy Gardner showed up at a neighbor's house with welts on her face. She told the neighbor her grandmother had abused her. But Wendy begged her not to call the authorities, saying she was afraid that if she complained, her grandmother would have her put into a group home.

When Betty Gardner called the neighbor looking for Wendy, the woman lied and said she hadn't seen her. She let Wendy stay with her the whole day.

Wendy told at least one other person that she had lived with the abuse for a long while. A television show the past year, she claimed, had showed her what abuse was and that it wasn't normal.

"Grams, that's what you do to us!" she recalled saying as the movie played.

Her grandmother had smacked her across the mouth.

The allegations of abuse, later repeated in court and to investigators, would become controversial in the succeeding months. Betty Gardner's sisters and others in the family vigorously denied that they were true. The accusations began after Betty started talking about putting Wendy into a group home, one sister said. Wendy's young sister Kathy also said they weren't true or were grossly exaggerated. Their father Buzz, however, told newspaper reporters they were true, one of many sore points between him and the rest of the family.

Not only was James' mother Dinah convinced they were true, but James' sister Donna, who as a trained emergency medical services worker was more than passingly familiar with signs of abuse, also believed the stories. And more.

Stopping by her mother's house one night, Donna found Wendy with a large slash on her wrists, apparently done by a sharp piece of glass. It looked to her as if the girl had attempted to commit suicide, though she couldn't be sure.

Though relatively petite herself, Donna towered over Wendy, and her forceful personality was something to be reckoned with in its own right. Her share of the family temper had been channeled by her profession; she had a direct manner and a clear head in emergencies. Grabbing the child, she cleaned the wound. Although it did not appear life-threatening, as she examined it, she realized it may not have been a suicide attempt at all. Nonetheless, she threatened to call the authorities. Wendy, who associated the attempt to her problems with her grandmother, begged her not to.

Unsure fully of what was going on, and aware that a complaint about abuse had been made, Donna held off. But she told Wendy this was the first and last time she would do such a thing. And she urged—begged, even—the girl to get professional counseling.

Rage and despair alternately percolated inside Wendy Gardner's chest as the December days grew shorter. Some part of her remained the little girl, anxious to please, aware that she was sinning. She cut herself a few times, trying to expiate her guilt by feeling pain. But there was no lasting relief; more and more she gave herself to the dark impulses, and ran to Evans for shelter and comfort.

Her grandmother continued to compare her to her mother. Wendy herself puzzled over her connection and inheritance. Torn by affection and hate, she wrote a letter late that fall which somehow found its way to the fetid apartment in the drug-infested area of Poughkeepsie where Jann Gardner lived.

The letter admitted that Jann still had a place in Wendy's heart. But it also said that Wendy felt she was no longer her mother. She used foul language, but not the worst she could muster. Even as she called the woman who had given birth to her a bitch, Wendy said she still might write to her again. Even as she wanted to slash her out of her life, erase her sins and genetic heritage, Wendy felt a tie that went beyond anything she could put into words, or even understand.

Jann tore up the letter and threw it into one of the fetid piles in the open lot behind her building.

"This guy has her controlled," Betty Gardner told herself when she woke a few days before Christmas. She blamed everything on Evans, feeling that he was manipulating her granddaughter against her.

As she set her feelings down on paper, Betty Gardner realized something else. She cared deeply for the young girl, but she had somehow lost the ability to talk openly and honestly to her about her concerns, at least in a way that would get through the shouting and tears. The gulf between them was too wide.

There was a moment there, jotting a few short notes in her small, crowded kitchen, when Betty Gardner regretted everything that had happened. Maybe it was a rush of self-realization, maybe it was the approaching Christmas season, but she seemed to hope that somehow, by some magic wand or maybe God's intercession, things would just snap together and everything would be all right. It was just a flash—she would yell at her granddaughter later the same day—but in her heart she hoped horribly for some kind of salvation.

Desperate to stop Wendy from following the path the girl's mother had taken, Betty Gardner did two things as Christmas approached that hurt her deeply.

The first was to begin formal proceedings in family court to have her granddaughter declared a "person in need of supervision." Commonly known as PINS, the procedure allows the court to intervene in rearing a child, generally to provide counseling or a structured environment, such as placement in a community home similar to the one James had gone to the year before. But contrary to what Betty and her granddaughter believed, placement in a community home is not a necessary or even general outcome of the process; in fact, even the formal filing of a PINS petition is comparatively rare. Most times, parents and guardians enter voluntarily into a program of treatment supervised by the probation department. The system is strongly prejudiced toward providing counseling, both formally and informally.

Betty Gardner had talked about sending Wendy to a group home and had threatened her with it for some time. As December crept on and Wendy became more and more unmanageable, she not only initiated the PINS procedure but worked diligently to bolster her case with notes on her behavior. Gardner told friends that a hearing had been set for early January; her comments to them made it apparent she believed it would result in Wendy being sent to the home, at least for a while.

As galling as it may have been for the older woman to admit her own flesh and blood was beyond her, Betty also considering taking what must have seemed an even more dire step, certainly one that ran against the grain of her strict Catholic upbringing. According to a close friend, as Christmas approached Betty discussed the possibility of helping her granddaughter obtain birth control pills. Aware that Wendy was having sex with Evans and powerless to stop it, she contemplated this lesser sin rather than have her granddaughter face an even more horrible future.

* * *

Evans and her daughter believed Wendy's stories of abuse. So did James. And the fifteen-year-old boy felt rage that someone was beating on his girlfriend. He heard the stories often, and though reluctant at first, he soon believed her as completely as he believed anything in his life.

His mother's solution was calling the authorities; James knew from experience how much good that did.

Tucked among the love notes from Wendy and later included in the court documents relating to her case is a short story James apparently wrote for school during the fall of 1994. It's unclear whether the story was ever submitted; the number 80 is circled at the top as if it was a grade, but there are no teacher's comments.

The lady kept screaming, so Neil raised his hand and smacked her across the face. She stopped yelling just long enough to punch him in the face and strike him with the flute and knocked him out. Neil woke up realizing he was tied to the bed. He started to yell, so the woman came up and said, "Shut up." Neil said, "What's your problem?" The old woman walked away, and slowly turned around and said, "You're pathetic." Neil squirmed loose and got free. He quickly ran away and got the truck running, never looking back.

III

JUST DO IT

6

"I want to kill her so bad"

Sunday evening, Dec. 25, 1994

No matter what the Christmas carols promised, it had been too warm for a white Christmas. Outside, the trees jabbed gray limbs against an austere, clouded sky. The church bells had long since faded, silence settling on the town as children finally exhausted the nervous energy that had driven them since early that morning. For most people the long day was sliding toward a peaceful ending; Christmas lights blinked on, their multi-colored glow already beginning to seem tired, maybe even jaded, marking the end of the holiday.

Wendy Gardner, sitting on James Evans' lap, hugged closer to her boyfriend. They had finished opening their presents earlier. James had bought Wendy a sexy black Spandex dress and gold earrings; Wendy had bought him a Walkman and a pair of pants. It had been a great holiday. They'd even talked again about getting married and living together forever, maybe in Puerto Rico. But now as night fell Gardner felt her insides churning. She hadn't been home all day. Her grandmother had recently filed a PINS petition in family court, which she worried would eventually mean she'd be put away in a group home, locked away from James and the only things that made her happy. She wasn't even supposed to be with him tonight, not on Christmas night, not on any night.

The whole family court thing was her grandmother's latest plot to keep them apart, Gardner thought. It wasn't going to work. She wouldn't let it. She would stay here as long as she wanted. *Fuck the bitch.*

For the past month, Wendy had practically lived in James' room. Some days she pretended to go to school, only to sneak back through the woods and come around to see him. Other days she didn't bother pretending at all.

They had sex whenever they wanted. They drank sticky-sweet wine coolers that made Gardner's head feel light and erased the last traces of pain.

The only thing between her and true happiness was her bitch grandmother with her damn PINS petition and her damn scheming to destroy a love that rocked. The old bag didn't know what love was, didn't understand the way an orgasm can explode inside you and change everything, the way snugging close to the chest of your boyfriend makes life silky smooth, Gardner thought. And she sure as hell didn't understand the way your body tingled when you told everyone to go to hell, the people who had looked down on you your whole life, who had excluded you, laughed at you behind your back. The dried up old hag didn't under-

stand the sheer fun of giving them the finger. She didn't
know what it was like to be young and alive, able to do
anything you wanted. Wherever, whenever, however,
right now and forever.

Wendy told Evans she would stay the night, as she
had so many times before. But James said it was Christmas, and between that and the PINS petition, she ought
to call and at least ask if it was OK.

Evans was odd that way. He would act like he didn't
give a rap about anybody, what they thought or did.
Then all of a sudden he'd surprise her with something
like, hey, it's Christmas, and she's your grandmother.

So Gardner went to the phone. Even as she dialed,
she felt her anger starting to build. She knew what Gram
was going to say.

Betty Gardner's voice came over the line. "Yes?
Hello?"

Somewhere, a Christmas carol was playing. Wendy
told her grandmother where she was, the words rushing
out as she asked to stay for the night.

"No," said Betty sharply. "I don't want you being
there at all."

The thin string that had held Wendy's emotions in
check snapped. "Fuck you, bitch," Wendy shouted.
"I'm staying here tonight no matter what you say."

She slammed down the phone. James looked at her
as her resentment spewed from her mouth. "She's such
a bitch. She's such a bitch. She's such a bitch."

James calmed her down. He was her comforter, just
like the song said. He had that key to her soul, the
warmth of his chest soothing her.

Call her again, he said. It's Christmas.

Her emotions were all tangled—resentment, anger,
something like longing to be accepted, something that

once felt like love. Wendy picked up the phone and re-dialed. She wanted to convince her grandmother. She thought she might if she just could find the right words. But her anger got away from her before Betty picked up. Wendy got the receiver back on the cradle, not waiting for a hello.

She calmed herself, dialed again. This time the phone rang and rang with no answer.

It was Christmas. James was right. Some part of the thirteen-year-old love-soaked rebel wanted to be the smiling cherub again; some part wanted only to be accepted and loved and hugged, even by the woman who stood between her and true happiness. Wendy picked up the phone once more and dialed the number, her fingers moving on their own.

Her grandmother's voice exploded over the line. "If you keep calling, I'm going to call the police."

The phone jostled in its cradle as Wendy Gardner flew into an uncontrollable rage. Whatever she had felt before was nothing compared to this. Words spewed from her mouth: bitch, grandma, they meant the same thing.

"I want to kill her," she said. "I want to kill her so bad. She's making me so angry."

Evans wrapped his arms around his lover. "She's making me angry, too," he said, trying to soothe her. "I love you, Wendy."

"I love you, too, but right now I'm not sure what that is."

"Will you marry me?"

"I will, but we're kind of young."

"Remember what I told you? We can go on a boat

five miles offshore and get married. As long as you're outside of the U.S."

"I want to, but I'm not sure," said Wendy. "I just— I just want to kill her."

James looked at her. "If I kill her, will you love me?"

"Yeah, but I don't think you'll do it."

"You want to bet?"

"I don't know, James. I still don't think you'll do it."

"After she kicked you down the stairs and everything, you still don't believe that I wouldn't kill her?"

"We'll have to see."

"Let's start planning."

They talked for a long time after that, talked and made love in the downstairs bedroom. Dinah Evans said later she spent most of the days around Christmas either out of the house or sick. She wasn't around to interfere and in any event the kids were careful to keep their whispers to themselves.

Talking about killing Betty Gardner had a strange effect on Wendy—it calmed her rage. She could be very logical, even about passionate murder.

If they were going to kill the old woman, how would they do it? A gun made sense, but they didn't have one.

"You got a point there," said James when Wendy pointed it out.

Maybe he could get one.

"Naw," said Wendy. That would take too long. They should just do it now, right now, before they had a chance to change their minds.

"Why don't we stab her?" she suggested.

"Too much blood," said Evans. "Why don't we snap

her neck? And if that doesn't work, we can try to choke her.''

''Yeah.''

So finally they had it, the perfect way to get rid of an old lady. It'd be easy.

But what would they do with the body?

Gardner suggested they chop it up into little pieces.

Evans was against it. There'd be too much blood.

Besides, did she really want to see someone's arm cut off? Or their head? Imagine her head chopped off and her eyes bulging.

Gardner agreed that was bad. No way.

They could burn her, Evans suggested. Nothing'd be left if they burned her.

Gardner thought that was a good idea.

But what if there wasn't enough time?

Evans suggested they just throw her in a ditch and let the body rot. By the time someone found her, she'd be rotted away to nothing.

Exhausted by a night of talking about murder and making love, the two teenagers slept late Monday, the day after Christmas. Dinah Evans wasn't around and there was no one to bother them as they lay together, making love again and again. Finally they decided to go outside for a walk. The conversation they had started earlier continued as they walked down the long block toward the shopping mall and the state highway, Route 9W. Every few steps something in the wind worried them and they feared someone might sneak up behind and overhear their plans.

The two lovers decided they could carry the dead body down the street in a wheelbarrow to the woods at the end of the block. They could use a sheet or something to cover the body. But Gardner realized someone in the houses lining the road might see them.

"What are they going to say if they see a sheet and a bag, a long bag and a wheelbarrow or something, or a dead body hanging out of it?" she asked.

Evans agreed it wouldn't work. They continued to debate as they passed the row of raised ranches and Cape Cods. It was quiet for a Monday, the subdivision close to deserted even though the weather wasn't bad for a winter day. Kids inside were playing with their new toys; a few had gone with their parents down to the mall to exchange gifts or maybe catch a movie.

Back at the house, Gardner told Evans the best thing they could do was throw grandma in her car trunk after they killed her.

"Yeah, I was thinkin' the same thing," answered James, sliding close and beginning to touch her breast. "OK. We're gonna do it."

"Yeah."

"Yeah."

The next day, Tuesday, came and went in a flash. They had stayed up late again, making love and talking and making love, and didn't finally wake up until four in the afternoon.

Wendy Gardner thought about the PINS petition, thought about how much she hated the bitch, how much she loved James. His little bedroom, with its posters and stuffed animals, its chair and its smell of him—Grandma wanted to wrestle her out of it, wanted to take everything important away from her. She thought about her and she hated her, and she wanted her dead all the more.

James Evans thought of Wendy getting beat up when she was little, and it made him angrier and angrier. And he thought of losing her, losing the thing that made him whole. No amount of sex, pushing himself into her again and again, could solve the ache he felt.

"I want to kill her so much," said Wendy.

"We're gonna do it," said James.

But instead they made love and hung out, and later walked down to the bowling alley not far from the house, and bowled and drank and talked about killing and came up with a plan. But they weren't murderers yet, just two kids without anybody watching them in a middle class house in the middle of a sleeping subdivision, groping for love in a tangle of blankets and dark emotion.

7

A damn personal way to die

Wednesday, Dec. 28, 1994

Early in the morning, so early the sky hung steel-gray above the house, the two teenagers woke from a fitful sleep. Groping turned to kissing and more; they rolled together and then fell apart. Anxiety fluttered in their stomachs, and before long they drifted not to sleep but talk.

"You really want me to do it?" James Evans asked.

"You won't do it," answered Wendy Gardner, "so I don't have to worry about it."

"I will if it means so much to you, that you will love me. I'll do anything for you, Wendy."

"Whatever," she mumbled, her eyes closing.

* * *

They didn't wake up again until mid-afternoon. By now they had a solid plan: they would go over to the house, strangle Grandma, then put her body in the trunk. Gardner had a speech all rehearsed: "You beat me, now it's your turn."

But what about Kathy, Wendy's sister, James had asked.

She should be out at religion class, Wendy told him. They'd do it before she got back.

Then what about when she came home?

Kathy wasn't going to like this, no way. They thought about the problem for a long while, unable to come up with a solution. They sat together, Gardner on Evans' lap, talking about what to do.

"We're not going to kill her," said Gardner. Evans didn't disagree, but he didn't want to get caught, either. Leave a witness around, and sooner or later you got caught. It always happened that way on TV.

"Why don't we tie her up in the attic?" Wendy suggested.

"Yeah, that might work," said James.

"When we tie her up you can fuck her instead of me 'cause I'm sick of you doing it to me all the time, especially when I don't want it," Gardner said.

"Yeah, I can."

"Anything, if you don't kill her."

"You know, we're going to have to kill her anyway."

"Yeah."

The day drifted on. Wendy Gardner went back and forth—she didn't want to kill Grams, she wanted to, she was afraid of James, she was eager to push him on. The times when James Evans wavered, she stoked him up; the times she worried they would be caught, he assured her he had it under control. The emotions made her head race, enshrouding the rest of the world in a dim, distant fog. Finally, she decided to call home, telling her grandmother she would stop by at six. The old lady wasn't very happy, but Wendy didn't much care. It no longer made any difference what Gram thought.

Were they really going to kill her?

Even if they didn't, Wendy wanted her Christmas presents. She had to go home sometime.

At six o'clock, Wendy dialed the number again. She was surprised when Kathy answered.

It was Christmas vacation. No school, not even for religion. Suddenly their plan was shot to hell.

Grandma came to the phone. Wendy stumbled and told her she'd be home later. She hurried to get off the phone.

"She's still there, James. Kathy is still there," said Gardner as she hung up. "What are we gonna do?"

"Let's kill her anyway. Let's just bring Kathy downstairs and tie her up so she doesn't run away."

"Let's, uh, let's wait a couple of hours, three hours, till Grandma goes downstairs," Gardner suggested. Her grandmother always watched TV in the basement rec room. It would be easier to kill her there, easier to drag her out to the garage from there. "I'm a little nervous about this, baby," she added.

"Don't be. It will all be over soon."

"I love you so much, James."

"I love you, too. That's all I wanted to hear. I'm gonna do it in about three hours."

After three more hours of making love, the two teenagers finally got ready to go out. James Evans had on his black Spalding sports pants, Nike sneakers, and a black t-shirt with a picture of the Tazmanian Devil, the Warner Brothers cartoon character who loved to torment Bugs Bunny. Wendy Gardner had her black sweatpants on. They threw coats over themselves and left the house.

Gardner carried a bag with the presents Evans had given her for Christmas. James brought along bluish-gray leather and canvas work gloves and a thin piece of nylon-reinforced kite string, about three feet long, looped at one soiled end, with the nylon beginning to fray in three separate strands at the other end.

It was well past nine by now. Betty Gardner was watching television in her usual spot, the downstairs rec room. She sat in a big old black chair that had been her husband's favorite.

The holidays wreaked havoc with the TV schedule. There was a special on with a slew of stars being honored, Kirk Douglas and Aretha Franklin among them, and a news program. Nothing that required a lot of thought.

At ten, *Law and Order* would come on NBC. Briscoe and Logan were supposed to help a young mother who claimed her baby was stolen shortly after birth.

And then there'd be the news, with its inevitable update on O.J. Simpson.

* * *

Appletree Drive curved around to meet Rose Lane practically in a straight line. Ordinarily it took no more than three minutes to walk from the Evans' front door to the Gardner's. Tonight the distance was endless, time seemed to run on forever. Before they had gone halfway there, Evans stopped in the middle of the road.

"Are we gonna do it?" he asked her.

"Yes. I want it done," she told him. "We plan too much. I want it over with."

"OK."

They started walking again. The night was clear, cold, but not so much that it took their breath away. Christmas lights flickered on and off throughout the neighborhood, tossing green and red snakes into the air, coloring the shadows on the ground with a dull orange fire. The couple had walked this particular stretch of asphalt hundreds of times over the past few months, but never with such deliberate steps.

They stopped in the Gardners' front yard. Through one of the basement windows they could see Grandma's legs in her polyester stretch pants, sticking out of the big black armchair. Grandma loved to lean back and scan through the channels.

"OK, James, let's go," said Wendy, leading the way to the door.

Inside in the kitchen, Kathy Gardner started when she heard the door open, then realized it was her sister. She tensed, knowing there would be a fight. The battles between Wendy and Grandma had reached epic proportions; she tried to stay out of them as much as possible.

So when Wendy came into the room and asked her to come downstairs to see the presents with their grandmother, she refused. Wendy insisted, and reluctantly, Kathy got up and followed her out past the living room to the landing. The Christmas tree stood nearby, a few boxes and presents scattered at it base. James was standing near the door, looking down toward the basement rec room.

They're going to tell Grandma they're getting married, the eleven-year-old suddenly thought.

That wasn't going to go over very big.

Downstairs, Betty Gardner had stopped paying attention to the TV. She put her glass of water on the side table and looked up from the armchair, anger boiling inside her. She'd gotten so many different opinions on how to handle her granddaughter that nothing made any sense any more. Kids these days didn't respect anything, not religion, not the sacrifices you made, not even the hard way the world was.

The times had gotten beyond her, beyond the anger that welled up when she heard Wendy's voice, beyond the disdain she felt when James Evans' long, gawky legs came down the steps of her house to her room.

Wendy walked across the room in front of the foldout couch and turned off the TV her grandmother had been watching.

"What's going on here?" Betty asked, getting up from her chair. Evans had on a pair of gloves—not winter gloves, but workman's gloves or the kind someone might use for pulling pricker bushes out of the yard.

Kathy hovered in the background, unsure what was going to happen.

Wendy shot James a glance. She had expected him to have jumped into action by now. But he didn't move. Nothing happened; their movements were all stiff and out of joint.

"We're gonna do what the plan says, right?" Evans asked her. He stood still, as if waiting for a switch to be thrown.

"What's going on here?" Betty Gardner asked again. This time, her tone was sharp and demanding.

"Shut up, it's none of your business," Evans barked.

"This is my house," said Betty, stepping toward him. "Get out!"

"Wendy, we're gonna do what the plan says, right?" said Evans. "Say what you have to say."

"Just do it," snarled Wendy Gardner as she grabbed her sister.

Kathy started to scream.

"Better be quiet," Wendy told her.

"Why? Why? What's going to happen?" asked the younger girl, panic and adrenaline streaming into her veins.

Betty tried to get around Evans, but he pushed her back. The glass flew to the floor, water spilling everywhere. Kathy Gardner began to kick and flail her elbows, but Wendy tightened her grip, pulling her toward the stairs, pulling her away from the storm that had erupted in the veneer-paneled family room.

Evans pushed Betty Gardner back with all his might as she tried to escape him. He grabbed her around the neck, both hands tightening. His anger leapt out of control, pumped by the ferocious rumble of his heart.

"Shut up, bitch!" he yelled as she tried to fight. He

saw black and red and the blue polyester of Betty's sweatshirt, saw the red plump curls of her hair, the white of her thick underpants as her shirt pulled up from the back as they struggled. He gripped his arms around her neck and yanked.

In the movies and television shows he had watched, an actor could pull back like this and a person's neck would snap. But they had it wrong—Betty Gardner only struggled harder.

"Remember this, bitch," he snarled through his teeth. "You're never going to be able to hit her again."

He pressed harder; this wasn't anywhere near as easy as he had thought it would be. For an old woman, Elizabeth "Betty" Gardner had a lot of fight.

No way he was going to lose this now. He was strong and he was determined. Somehow Evans got the kite string out and around her neck, then put his foot on her back. He was behind and he had all the leverage and time, lots of time—time was on his side, no matter how else the odds were stacked.

Maybe in that moment, as the prosecutor would later say, Betty Gardner was just an obstacle to what James Evans desired, her granddaughter's undying love. Or maybe, as a defense psychiatrist would later contend, she was a villain he had to vanquish so his lover would be safe, the latest in a line of abusers trying to destroy the only thing that made James real. Or maybe she had become the embodiment of every bitter thing that James Evans had ever faced—every rejection, every beating, every punishment, every disappointment, every denial, every fist slamming against his face in the dark cold of the night.

Maybe she had taken the shape of the demons that had haunted him, in dreams and in reality.

Whatever Betty Gardner was, James Evans curled the fingers of his right hand around the thin string on her neck and pulled taut. He held on.

8

"Jingle Bells"

Wednesday, Dec. 28, 1994 Continued

While James Evans struggled with her grandmother, Wendy Gardner clamped her hand over Kathy Gardner's mouth and dragged her upstairs, trying to keep her quiet. The eleven-year-old did not go passively. Wendy had to slap and kick her. She smashed her sister's head into the wall before she finally got her upstairs to the living room, past the Christmas tree to the couch.

"If you don't stop screaming," Wendy threatened, "he'll kill you, too."

Finally, Kathy quieted down. Tears kept exploding from her eyes, rage, grief, and disbelief tangled in a knot. "Why did you have to do this?" she asked. "Why did this have to happen?"

"Don't you remember what she did to us when we were younger?" Wendy asked. "How she beat us?"

"She didn't beat us."

Wendy's eyes flared with anger as her sister denied they had ever been mistreated. "She beat us," the older girl raged. "She kicked us down the stairs and smashed us into walls. I think that's called beating." She turned and looked back past the Christmas tree to the iron railing above the stairs. "James, is it done?"

"Not yet. I'm almost done," he called back. "She's starting to piss herself."

Kathy began shaking uncontrollably. She found a Bible nearby. Desperately, she tried reading the words, hoping there might be a miracle, or comfort at least.

As the screaming downstairs turned to moans, Wendy began to sing "Jingle Bells," drowning out the sounds. It was Christmas, after all.

"Is it done?" Wendy Gardner called down when she realized it was quiet.

There was a thump on the thinly carpeted cement floor. Gardner looked at a clock and felt the time burn into the retinas of her eyes—9:58 P.M.

"Yeah, she's gone," Evans called up.

He appeared in the hallway, strange red ink scrawled on his arm and hands, writing Wendy couldn't decipher. She got up and followed him into the kitchen.

"What's on your arm?" she asked.

"Probably the juice that she had." Evans took off the gloves.

"She didn't have juice. She had water. That isn't juice."

"Yeah," he said, taking off the gloves and staring at them. Something clicked and he realized what the stain was. "It's blood. When I choked her, after I tried to snap her neck and it didn't work, I tried choking her with the kite string and it closed up her throat and she started bleeding.''

"I thought there wasn't going to be any blood.''

"Well, her throat swelled up. I didn't think that was going to happen.''

"She's dead, she's dead, she's really dead.''

"Be quiet, baby. Everything's all right.'' Evans folded his wet arms around her, hugging her against the picture of the cartoon character on his chest. "She's dead now, she won't ever hurt you.''

"Did she say anything to you before she was dead?''

"Nothing but *uhhhhh.*''

"Oh God.''

It took forever to get the blood off his arm. James Evans scrubbed it and soaked it, ran it under the water again and again, got the skin practically water-logged, and still the blood and its indecipherable message stayed. For the longest time it seemed the bitch had burned a last message into his flesh.

When they calmed down, Evans and Gardner went to look at the body. Betty's corpse sprawled on the thin, worn, industrial carpet, its beige threads stained with dark brown blood. The television was pushed off to one side; a small table with a telephone sat nearby. Wendy couldn't believe that her grandmother was truly, finally dead.

Evans dragged the body out to the garage. He didn't stop when Betty's canvas sneaker fell off, just hauled her out in a lump. Back upstairs, Wendy again talked with Kathy about how their grandmother had abused them. Kathy insisted it wasn't true. Wendy kept getting angrier and angrier, but when James came back she told him not to hurt Kathy; he could tie her up instead.

There was no need to. Evans saw Kathy was spazzed out and wouldn't do anything. The two teenagers left her in her room and went to get rid of the evidence. With a steak knife they sawed apart the bloodstained rug, rolling up a long strip and putting it into a large plastic garbage bag. As murders go, it wasn't a huge amount of blood, but it seemed like gallons to them.

Then James—*Jame$*—remembered the money. Wendy hunted around for her grandmother's pocketbook. She found it downstairs on the couch, lying within a few feet of where Betty Gardner had been murdered. Wendy brought it upstairs by the Christmas tree and tore it open. There was about $400: a fortune.

"We'll probably have to find an apartment," Wendy said to James.

"I don't know if I'm old enough to find one," he replied.

"We'll have to call around tomorrow."

There must be more money in the house somewhere, they thought. Gardner got up and led Evans to her grandmother's bedroom. She tried to avoid her reflection in the dresser mirror as she hunted for cash. In a small box they found another stash of bills, bringing their total take to $883. James grabbed it and held it out to her nose, smiling.

"Smell it," he said. "Smell it."

Continuing to hunt through the room, Gardner came upon an old photo album. Thinking there might be more money in it, she took it to the bed and began flipping through.

She found pictures instead, pictures of when she was

a little baby, pictures of her with her grandmother at Christmas time years before, an old, old picture of her father and grandmother, smiling, a blissful moment before hate fell between them.

Wendy started to cry. James reached up and put his arm around her, her comforter again, calming her.

She got back up and went to the dark, boxy dresser, no longer looking for money, seeking out pictures instead. She buried herself in a pile of them at the edge of the bed, looking and remembering, wandering through guilt and fear and anger.

"She's dead," Gardner sobbed. "I loved her, James. I don't understand why I actually thought that you'd kill her after a while."

Evans stared at her, bewildered. It was late now, very late.

"You don't look like a killer to me, James," Wendy told him. "I can't understand how you could do something like that."

"I guess you don't know me totally," he said in disbelief. "You don't know most of me."

"I wish I never met this part of you."

"Well, you did. Now you're stuck with me."

Wendy started to sob again.

Evans left her with the pictures and went to check on Kathy. She was half-sleeping.

He told her they had found money. She could have a hundred and fifty dollars.

She told him no.

He left her in her room.

It was well past midnight before Wendy Gardner gave up looking at the photos and went back downstairs with

Evans, back down to the room where he had strangled her grandmother. The rug they had cut away made a jagged line in front of the couch, a finger of death pointing toward the paneled wall. Betty Gardner still lay a few feet away, beyond the thick garage door. They opened the sleep-out couch and pulled some blankets together, got on the bed, bare inches from the spot on the floor where Evans had choked the life from Betty Gardner.

Wendy lay down, sleep starting to creep up her spine. But something kept it at bay.

Her grandmother's eyes from the other room, eating through the wall.

Evans felt them too.

"It's making me sick knowing that she's laying in the garage facing us, staring at us," said James.

"That's it," snapped Gardner. "We got to get rid of that body somehow."

Evans nodded, but already his hands were sliding over her breasts and down her belly. "We will. After we have some sex."

9

"Killers Don't Cry"

Thursday, Dec. 29, 1994

Out of nowhere, Wendy Gardner put down the controller for the Super Nintendo game and began to cry. "I can't believe it happened," she sobbed. "I still can't believe it happened. Why did it have to happen? Why did it have to happen?"

James Evans clung to her. Tears were coming from his eyes, too.

"I'm a killer," he said. "I didn't want to really do it, but I did it for you, baby. I love you so much."

It was still early, barely past seven-thirty. They'd already had breakfast. James hadn't slept much, grabbing only snatches of rest in a crazed patch of confusing images. During the night, Betty Gardner had loomed from darkness in his dreams, alive again, her face twisting like a ghoul's Halloween mask.

"You're worthless!" she screamed at him in his fitful sleep. "Worthless!"

Even though he was awake now, he felt the fear again. Evans trembled for a moment, nearly losing control. Then he sat straight back, gathered himself, remembered the role he had to play.

"Killers don't cry," he told Gardner, making his face into a stoic mask. "So I might as well stop."

They'd drifted into unconsciousness after making love. In the middle of the night Wendy couldn't sleep; her grandmother's eyes seemed to be staring at her through the wall. They'd gotten up to put the body in the trunk of the car.

"Stupid bitch," Evans had said to the prostrate body before bending down to pick up his end. He kicked her in the head, hard.

Grams was dead all right. She didn't move. And she was heavy.

There was blood on the old woman's neck. The string had cut a thin, deep circle, as if James Evans had been trying to decapitate her. Now in the trunk, her sweatshirt bunched up to her shoulders, exposing the plump, white skin of her back and the roll of fat at her stomach. The old woman's breasts sat in the hub of the worn spare tire, her mouth resting on an empty cola can. Her rump twisted up from her knees and one shoeless foot poked into the wheel well. An ice scraper sat a few inches from the red curls of her hair.

The trunk was immaculate, as if it had been vacuumed hours before, as if she'd gotten it ready.

* * *

Evans and Gardner had talked about suicide when they were planning the murder. In the dim light of early morning James saw that Wendy had a scissors in her hand, she was cutting herself. Whether it was suicide or purification, Evans went crazy. He grabbed the scissors and shook her. They weren't going to kill themselves, weren't going to hurt themselves.

Not now.

What do you do after you've murdered someone, had sex, and slept almost on the spot where you killed them? What do you do after you've set yourself free, with nearly nine hundred bucks hot in your pocket and no one around to keep you back?

James Evans and Wendy Gardner decided to treat themselves to a pizza for lunch at the Pizza Hut in the Great American Mall on the state highway, about a ten-minute walk away. They took Kathy, who seemed to be in a walking daze, with them. It was warm for December, with a clear sky; by the middle of the afternoon the temperature would edge toward the fifties. It had been like that all week, one of the warmest starts to winter on record.

Before they left, Evans snuck back to his house for fresh clothes. Along the way he met Barry Green, who ended up going with them to the restaurant. Green didn't know he was walking with two murderers, and beyond the looks and giggles that passed between them, they didn't let on. He didn't realize when he played his gangsta rap tapes for them—Snoop Doggy Dogg's

Doggystyle with "Murder Was the Case," and Grave-diggaz "6 Feet Deep"—how ironic they were.

Evans liked the music. A lot of people did.

It began to feel like a party. Pizza, and then a spree at the grocery store—soda and munchies and just about anything a kid could want. They got back to the house and the car was still there, with the body in the trunk, but that reality was fading as another took hold. For the first time in their lives, Evans and Gardner had actual roles to play: killers. The instructions were all laid out in the raps and songs they listened to that afternoon: you partied, flashed your gold, and fucked bitches. Death was a righteous rite, put out by special people, celebrities in an otherwise bland and blander world. Killers pushed things to the far edge, and off.

There was an undercurrent in the music that Evans was attracted to, a theme even stronger than the talk about killing and partying. The heroes of the songs were all trapped in their situations, ratted out by fate or destiny, dealt a bad "case." When Snoop Doggy Dog rapped on "Murder Was the Case," the point wasn't that the hero had committed murder—which someone who didn't know the music might infer from the title— but that the hero was murdered. He was trapped in a stoic, sad, ultimately love-starved life. No matter how big your machine gun or how bad your bitch, the songs said, you were nailed. Unable to escape, heroes carried on with their assigned roles, waiting for the inevitable.

Sometime in the afternoon, James Evans decided to try driving the car. Barry Green, who never learned about the murder, left. They took Kathy and headed over to the bowling alley to meet another friend, Andy Bender, who was bowling there.

Evans was still a few weeks shy of sixteen, when he would be old enough to get a driver's license in New York. But driving Betty Gardner's big old Mercury wasn't all that hard. He was nervous about it at first, and stuck to the small, quiet network of roads in the neighborhood. By nightfall—the sun set around four-thirty—he was screeching the tires, leaving rubber, pulling what the teenagers called "burnouts" on the road and lot in front of the bowling alley. Rocks and pebbles from the parking lot flew in all directions.

Some kids at the bowling alley saw him and came over to Gardner and Evans when they walked out to go for another ride. They had left Kathy inside with Andy Bender, trusting her not to run away or tell anyone what they had done.

"I thought you were fifteen," said one of them.

"So?" answered James.

"How can you drive?"

"I can drive."

"Where'd you get the car?"

"I stole it."

The other kids started to laugh. Evans smirked. Gardner told him to blast it.

The Mercury rocketed forward, Grandma still locked in the trunk. Dirt and stones whipped out behind them, scattering the youths, who thought it was all great fun. Evans tightened his hands around the wheel, coasting behind the Great American mall. There was a row of dumpsters there, angled haphazardly along the macadam border of the roadway. He gunned for them, foot stomping down on the gas.

"I'm gonna kill us," he said.

"No, not while people are watching," said Wendy, grabbing for the dashboard, for the door handle, for anything to brace herself as the big car lurched across the road, out of control. "Not yet, not yet."

They went back to the house, where James got his bowling ball. They came back and spent more time bowling.

For Kathy Gardner, the day must have had a surreal quality, terror mixed with the sort of things an eleven-year-old would do on a birthday. Her sister had threatened her with death. So had James Evans. Kathy had already heard Evans kill her grandmother. Wendy had explained exactly how they had planned the murder. At times the pair seemed to trust her completely, leaving her alone in the bowling alley and not bothering to tie her up the night before. At other times, they watched her as closely as a squad of jail guards would watch a prisoner.

"How does it feel to be with two murderers?" her sister asked, like it was all a joke.

The answer was more complicated than words.

Kathy Gardner later told investigators that at two the morning after the murder, she had woken up to strange sounds downstairs. Maybe hoping that everything had just been a bad, bad dream, she had gotten out of bed and started to go down to the basement rec room. But as she reached the stairs, she had heard Wendy moan in ecstasy. She and James were just having sex.

Transfixed, Kathy had stood there, unable to move until Wendy had called to her from below. One or both of them had taken a step toward each other before Kathy had realized her sister was nude.

Wendy had called to her to come on down. "You've seen me naked before."

Kathy had told her no, and gone back to bed.

Now, back at the bowling alley, she worried about what would happen next. Left there with fourteen-year-old Andy Bender, she was petrified that her sister and James might return at any second. She was too scared to say anything, though she wanted to.

She was shocked when Bender told her he knew about her grandmother being dead. A friend of James' had come by with a gun and blew her away, he said. James had told him everything.

No, Kathy said carefully. That wasn't the way it happened at all.

Andy Bender wasn't exactly the kind of person most people would confide in. Reckless at best, the youth seemed to have a crazy and unpredictable streak; later, he would end up having his own minor scrapes with the law and an assistant district attorney would call him crazy. Like many of Evans' friends, he was younger than Evans and some years older than Kathy Gardner. But she set him straight anyway. He was all she had.

He listened, surprise registering on his face. Then he told her he understood. He was scared for her.

After Gardner warned Bender that she would kill him if he did anything to Kathy, who was still a virgin, Gardner and Evans let them walk back to the house together.

They ended up walking around and talking for nearly an hour. Both were worried about what would happen to them, and what they should do. When Andy told Kathy to run away, she said she was too scared. James and Wendy would find her and kill her, too.

By now, Bender was positive Mrs. Gardner was dead

because Evans had shown him the body, but it would never be precisely clear what else he believed, how scared he was, or how he thought the murder occurred. Finally, he returned with Kathy to the house.

Downstairs, James, Wendy and Andy fooled around, then dozed off on the pull-out bed. Around one, Wendy got up and went upstairs, desperate for a bath. She soaked and scrubbed herself, cleaning every inch of her flesh.

By the time she was done, Evans and Bender were awake and hungry. Someone suggested going to the diner. But there was a problem—what to do with Kathy. None of the rooms in the house could be locked from the outside.

Bender volunteered to help Evans solve the problem. The "lock" they came up with was nothing more than some string and a light bulb tied between two doorknobs. If someone tried to open the door, the string would snap taut and the light bulb would break.

Maybe.

Kathy, already half-asleep, remained in the room for the rest of the night.

There was no rap music on the jukebox at the Barclay Heights diner, though the offerings ran from Aerosmith to Sinatra. A middle-class, low-key joint with thick burgers and friendly help, it wasn't the prime spot for a killer's breakfast, but it was all that was open.

It was rarely busy at this hour and the service was swift. A waitress appeared from nowhere, spooking them as she asked what they wanted.

Gardner, Evans, and Bender ordered nearly $34

worth of food—not easy in a place where a deluxe burger plate with fries goes for five bucks. They ordered burgers and roast beef and as much as they wanted as several hundred bucks were still hot in their pockets.

They left almost all of the food on their plates. The center of Evans' hamburger looked too much like red blood.

So did the lights on the police car that suddenly passed by on the state highway, just outside.

Another passed, lights flashing. It stopped in front of the diner. A road block was being set up nearby.

Panicking, Wendy, James, and Andy left their money and tried to get out as calmly as possible, hearts thumping so loud it was as if a drum machine was running. Back in the car, Evans turned the key as the others held their breaths. For a second, pulling out onto the highway, it seemed as if the cops were coming for them.

Evans floored it in the opposite direction, flying down the road a few hundred yards, then sailing right onto Simmons Boulevard near the plaza without signaling, as if that might fool pursuers. They slashed around to Appletree, zooming toward their house. Wendy was sure Kathy had escaped and called the cops.

Grandma lay silent in the trunk, the empty cola can rolling against her face as the car bounced back and forth in the hands of its inexperienced driver.

Bender got out near Rose Lane to scout for them and warn them if the cops were waiting. But by the time they turned the corner it was obvious no one was there except Kathy, asleep in her bed. The police had been working a traffic accident; it had nothing to do with them.

* * *

There was no way to calm down after that. It was as if they'd each taken ten hits of speed. The adrenaline ran through their veins like a rocket heading for Mars.

The body was still in the trunk. The best thing to do was to get rid of it somewhere, they decided; they had to hide the evidence. No sense taking any more chances. James Evans and Wendy Gardner decided to find a place to get rid of it.

Problem was, no one wanted to sit in the backseat, next to the body. Grandma's head was facing that way, her eyes squinting toward the murderers.

Andy Bender suggested Palenville, a Catskill mountain town with vast open places, wooded hillsides, and more than its share of forgotten ditches. Less than ten miles away from downtown Saugerties, the drive was a straight-at-the-mountains shot up Route 32. The Catskills shimmered with the reflected light of the stars and moon. Headlights would hunt up odd shadows from the fields or an occasional deer, but for the most part, the road was deserted.

The car climbed at a steady pace, aiming for the stars. Here and there an old wreck half-hidden in someone's yard loomed in the pale light, a reminder of the inevitable progress of time, the inevitability of growing old and getting used. To be alone in this mountain area is to be truly alone, without comfort, family or friends. The trio huddled together against the cold, the thrill of driving and even the adrenaline starting to fade.

More than a hundred years before, around the time of Saugerties' heyday, the eastern Catskills were a major tourist attraction, a place for weary New Yorkers to escape to. They came by stagecoach, boat, and later train, riding the final leg on bumpy coaches to the fresh, cleansing air overlooking the mighty Hudson. The Catskill House was the most famous hotel, perched above North Lake, but there were countless others. The region was made famous by painters like Thomas Cole, Frederick Church, and Samuel Morse, practitioners of the Hudson River School of painting. They were America's Romantics, existentialists who found God in nature, celebrating the eternal power in their paintings of dark forests and valleys lit by a single, overwhelming light.

Their history has faded now. The eastern Catskills are still popular with hikers and winter skiers, but the rush ended decades ago, even before airplanes brought other destinations into vogue. Nearly all the old resorts, even the once-famous Catskill House, are gone, razed or simply collapsed into dust. All that remains are the mountains, solid as ever, shouldering the sky like silent vanguards of judgment.

There must be a million places to dispose of a body on the roads that wind, sometimes in dirt, through the area. With luck, the crows would pick a body apart before the end of winter. It is not inconceivable that Betty Gardner's profaned body, tossed a mere hundred or so yards off an obscure trail, would have gone unnoticed for centuries. Others have.

But somehow, Evans and Gardner could never find the right place to dump her. They could never find the guts to open the trunk and look at the body again, feel its weight in their hands, wet their skin with its blood.

To go beyond Palenville is to climb directly into the sky. Mountains run straight up from the pavement; the moon slides toward you as the road curves. For one brilliant moment, the pale disc seems to come right down to you, warm and cheerful.

But James Evans and Wendy Gardner could find no solace there. For in the role of killer, a person gives up more than the ability to cry, more than the ability to wonder at the majesty of nature and the awesomeness of the mountains.

The old Mercury balked, the transmission groaning as it downshifted to take the ever-steepening grade. It seemed not to want to run away. The darkened landscape became harsh. The road that just moments ago seemed dry and safe turned against them, narrowing and narrowing, becoming increasingly difficult to navigate. The thick stone walls along the highway leaned in, anxious to extract revenge. On the right-hand side of the car, a stream raged over an immense falls; the sound penetrated the car with an eerie roar.

The roadway had become impassable, every turn designed to throw them off the side, toss James and Wendy, not the body they carried behind them, into the horrible, gaping ravines.

Finally, Evans found a place to turn around. They retreated back to Saugerties, to safety, grandma's body still locked in the trunk of the car.

10

Nothing Better to Do

Friday, Dec. 30, 1994

Friday was another warm day, sun mixed with clouds, temperatures quickly climbing into the forties. Kathy woke to find Wendy and James filling the car with soda, candy, bags of potato chips, and snacks.

"We're leaving," Wendy told her. "Take whatever you need. We're not coming back."

The eleven-year-old didn't believe her. Instead of packing clothes, she took her teddy bears.

Wendy took a teddy bear, too.

She also took the plastic garbage bag which contained the bloody rug she and Evans had cut off the basement floor. They drove over to the back of the Great American Mall, where Gardner got out and tossed the bag into a dumpster. They hung out for a while, going into the drug store and the Jamesway department store, shopping aimlessly. Hungry, they drove down to the McDonald's a short distance away. Kathy told them she didn't want anything so they left her alone in the car.

Watching them through the window, Kathy Gardner debated what to do. The highway was nearby, the diner just across the street. A group of houses sat behind the restaurant separated by the parking lot and a fence.

Help seemed far off; still, this might be her only chance.

Slowly, carefully, Kathy opened the door and began walking away.

Suddenly, she heard running. Wendy had seen her and was running to catch her.

For a long second, Kathy stood frozen in the parking lot. Finally her legs started moving again, but it was too late. Her sister grabbed her.

Kathy started to struggle, but Wendy calmed her down by saying that she and James had been talking about letting her go. Finally, Kathy let Wendy take her back to the car.

They were bored, James and Wendy. The bowling alley wasn't open, and there was nothing more they wanted to buy at the local Jamesway. They'd already gorged themselves at the supermarket, and the Great American plaza held little else of any interest. Eventually Evans just decided, fuck it. They were going to get caught sooner or later anyway—why not live it up in the meantime? Why not go down to the Hudson Valley Mall, a real shopping mall with real stores? They could have some fun there; they had the bucks.

* * *

The drive down Route 9W from Saugerties to the mall took no more than twenty minutes. There was a stretch on the highway where the road ran in an unbroken straight line, where for a moment it felt like no one, nothing, was ever going to stop them. Where everything felt perfect.

Evans bought a Dallas Cowboys football jersey with star running back Emmett Smith's number on it. The Super Bowl was coming up, and it looked like America's Team was going to win again. Gardner got a shirt, too. At J.C. Penney's, Wendy bought some sexy bras and some lingerie. They wandered down the midway toward the food court, stopping in a music store so Evans could buy his own Snoop Doggy Dog and Grave Diggaz tapes. The music stayed with him, a vibrant soundtrack rapping out the killer's role as he flashed his cash and basked in the glow of Wendy's love.

People who met them that day saw they were serious lovers. A clerk later marveled at how hooked they were on each other, so in love they had to have the exact same kind of sneakers, Reebok cross-trainers. They hugged and kissed, leaning into each other, sharing a secret that made them both more dangerous than they had ever dreamed of being.

James and Wendy, Wendy and James—they played together in the arcade, ate in the food court, strolled through the gaudy hallway of the mall on a wild spending spree, enjoying themselves as they never had before. By the time they left the mall that afternoon, Kathy in tow, they had only a bit more than a hundred dollars of Grandma's money left.

Betty Gardner's body was still in the trunk, silent eyes staring through the metal and fabric of the old Mercury.

Neither Evans nor Gardner felt much like going home, but there was little else to do. They drove up to Saugerties, into the village, across the bridge overlooking the falls that had made the town in the first place. The name Saugerties came from the old word "sawyer", and had to do with a sawmill set up along one of the creeks back in the days when white men were scared to go too far from the major river settlements and their guns. There are tales of Indian slaughters along these solid rocks, of whites getting murdered and natives getting slaughtered. Most of the stories seem more tall tales than truth, but there's blood in the ground here, sure enough.

There's also serenity, a small lake beyond the falls where James Evans and Wendy Gardner spent the last light Friday afternoon watching the ducks.

When they finally got home, they were relieved and maybe a little surprised to find that the police had not arrived. Evans had thought they'd be nailed by now.

None of the neighbors and none of their relatives had yet found it odd that Betty Gardner wasn't around. Although Kathy had made plans to see a great aunt and her father, no one suspected the reason those plans had been changed.

Things on Appletree Drive, Saugerties, New York, settled down into a peaceful routine for the night. Wendy and James went downstairs to play with video games they'd gotten that afternoon, NBA Jam and Streetfighter II, and each other. Then Kathy, James, and Wendy started watching television. Tired from all they had done over the past few days, Gardner and Evans eventually fell back on the thin mattress of the fold-out couch, exhausted. Kathy, after dozing off, went up to her room and went to bed.

The weather reports for the next day said there might be snow; a growing chill was expected. The two lovers had not yet worked out a plan, had not yet quite decided what to do. There were so many questions:

What should they do about the body?

What should they do about Kathy?

What would they say if someone came by and asked where Grandma was?

What if the police came?

What if Andy told on them?

Snoop Doggy Dog and Grave Diggaz had no answers for them, none that were optimistic, anyway. The only hints from the music and the movies were fatalistic, dark and foreboding. Like running yourself into a brick wall, or lying down as the guns went off. If murder was your case, you were in for it, no matter what you did.

The foreboding faded as they lay on the mattress, huddling together against the basement's damp air. Tomorrow was time enough. Tomorrow had all kinds of possibilities. Tomorrow they might run away, go beyond the mountains and the malls, start a new life as husband and wife. Tomorrow they might finally gather enough courage to dump the body, then conjure some story about strange men robbing them. Tomorrow they might let Kathy go, or maybe just kill her, too. Tomorrow they might burn the place down, like Wendy had seen in a movie once, burn it and let the body go up in flames, disguising their crime. Tomorrow they might wake up and be Bonnie and Clyde, two young lovers striving out on a suicide run for fame, gore, and a storybook end.

There were so many possibilities tomorrow. They were still young. Their future lay ahead.

11

Escape

Saturday, Dec. 31, 1994

Kathy Gardner woke up around seven o'clock in the morning on Saturday, December 31, the last day of 1994. She sneaked down the hallway, past the Christmas tree, down the stairs, beneath the print of wild horses running free, down past the landing to the rec room. Her sister and Evans were both asleep.

She wanted to escape. She knew she had to run away. But what if no one believed her story? Worse, what if James or Wendy heard, and ran after her?

Was it more scary to stay, or to run away?

She went back to her room, still unsure what to do.

For close to four hours, she debated. Her fear rose and fell. Her instincts for survival argued with her sense of justice.

Finally, sometime around eleven o'clock in the morning on New Year's Eve, the eleven-year-old put a thin jacket over her pajamas and slipped out of the house. She ran barefoot down the road, across to where some friends lived. Not waiting to catch her breath, she told the neighbors that her grandmother had been killed and stuffed in the trunk of her car, which was just now sitting in the driveway of the house a short distance away.

One part of her nightmare was over. The greater part would never leave her.

IV

A BODY IN THE TRUNK

12

Not here

Saturday, Dec. 31, 1994 Continued

Sitting in the cramped radio room at the Saugerties town police headquarters, the dispatcher wheeled around in his chair as the call came in. Until now, it had been an uneventful day, as most were. With thirteen full-time patrolmen and two detectives, the twenty-year-old department mostly handled accidents and minor crimes. Every month, something between 100 and a 150 tickets were written up; 14,000 miles rolled across the odometers of the force's half-dozen or so patrol cars, depending on the state of the town budget. The big action that year had been Woodstock '94, but that was long over. Like small squads throughout the country, the town cops were mostly a deterrent, a presence. Serious crimes such as big-ticket robberies, major drug deals, or anything that even looked like a homicide, were left for the state troopers over at the Kingston barracks, about twenty minutes away. The things the locals did fell into familiar, routine categories.

But the call that came in at 11:14 A.M. over the Ulster County 911 system, flagged to the Saugerties headquarters by a central dispatching system, was anything but routine. A young girl had told neighbors that her sister and boyfriend had killed her grandmother and stuffed the dead woman's body in a car trunk.

Even if the dispatcher might have been tempted to consider the call a joke, the location of the incident sounded an ominous note. For the Gardner name wasn't unknown in that small office. Betty Gardner had called often over the past few months, speaking to various department members, including the chief. She was having trouble with her granddaughter and her granddaughter's boyfriend. The police had handled some minor calls with kids in the area. The chief, a former juvenile officer, had advised Mrs. Gardner to file a PINS petition to try and get a hold on Wendy Gardner.

Still, when it went out over the radio, in Saugerties, in upstate New York, on an overcast, chilly day, the last day of the year, the alert sounded just a bit overblown.

Kill someone? There hadn't been a murder in town for at least a decade, maybe more.

Kill your grandmother?

Not here.

Saugerties Sergeant George Heidicamp was among the first on the scene, turning the car down the long road about a mile from the police station. There was nothing on the outside of the house on Appletree Drive that looked suspicious, nothing on the block or in the entire neighborhood that made it any different than any other middle-class enclave in a quiet town. Christmas decorations were strung in the windows, the front light was on, and the curtains drawn. A wreath with a bright red bow hung on the door, and dried up flowers sat at the edge of the driveway. Betty Gardner's car was sitting in the driveway.

Was there a body in there? Not in the back or front seats. Some clothes, candy, soda bottles, junk—but no body, no blood.

No one seemed to be moving inside the house. It might all be a hoax, or a figment of someone's overworked imagination.

Other Saugerties officers arrived. Detective Henry Mirabella, a tough, no-time-for-small-talk cop got out of his car. Someone went around to the back while others knocked on the front door. There was no answer.

The door in the back wasn't locked.

Inside the house, James Evans stumbled into consciousness. Someone was banging on the front door, banging all around.

"We gotta get out, we gotta get out," he shouted, bolting toward the garage. He was dressed in a pair of silk boxer shorts decorated with pictures of Bugs Bunny, Daffy Duck, and the Tazmanian Devil.

The police were already coming in. Police were everywhere, more police than Evans thought possible.

Naked and dazed with sleep, Wendy Gardner pulled a blanket around herself. James was already talking to the cops, saying nothing had happened. One of the police officers was asking where her grandmother was. She mumbled that she didn't know.

The town police brought the two young lovers upstairs. Evans asked one of the officers if he could get dressed. The officer shrugged and James went for some clothes. He brought back a sweatshirt for Wendy, whose teeth were starting to chatter from the cold.

Outside, Detective Mirabella paused before popping open the trunk of the 1984 Mercury.

This wasn't the sort of crime you wanted to think took place here, not at Christmas, not on New Year's Eve, not ever.

The trunk lid came up. And beneath the cement-white sky of the cold December day, there was no way anyone could deny what had happened.

Someone called the state police.

13

Timeline

When it was done, the case would seem as if it snapped together like a preschooler's jigsaw puzzle, a paint-by-numbers exercise designed to pad police resumes.

But it didn't start that way. In the chaos of the moment, there were at least a dozen priorities, and a hundred different ways to proceed.

Called in from his Ulster County home, State Police Bureau of Criminal Investigation Lieutenant Steven Nevins jumped in his car and headed for Saugerties. He made out a duty roster in his head as he drove, mentally assigning different tasks to different people, lining up who ought to be working where. Three senior investigators were already on their way to Saugerties. He had a good man in nearby Kingston, Senior Investigator Eddie Collins, a veteran of over twenty-five years and one of the most well-respected senior investigators in the troop, if not the entire force. A taciturn cop's cop— don't call him grizzly to his face—Collins could be counted on to get the ball rolling right away.

Nevins, an athletic man with a firm grip and a cocky smile, was responsible for investigators in two counties besides Ulster, as well as the Troop F forensics identification unit. Given to wearing crisp khakis, an immaculate white shirt, and serious ties, he cut a recruiting-poster Tom Cruise image—*Top Gun* in a blue and gold troop car. He'd come up the ladder quickly, with all the marks of a comer. Starting in uniform in 1981, he'd made sergeant by 1987 and gone over to BCI in 1988. He'd worked narcotics—then as now a sure road to advancement, or a wooden box. Back in uniform as a zone commander for a brief stint, he'd started his present assignment the previous January. Most of the men who worked for him called him an excellent supervisor. Tough, they said, but always fair, a guy who would stand behind you, and also let you know about it if you screwed up.

By now a dozen or so investigators were rushing to the scene, all hand-picked by Nevins or his senior investigators. On a major crime like this, the "bosses" called in people from all of the barracks in the surrounding area, people they'd worked with before and come to count on, people whose skills and foibles they knew better than those of their wives. You didn't screw around on a homicide.

The New York State Police agency, known universally as the State Troopers, began in 1913 after a Westchester man was attacked by robbers and fatally wounded while delivering a payroll to his boss. His employer, Miss Moyca Newell, went to the local part-time constable, hoping he could capture the robbers. The man, a grocer, wouldn't risk his own life, and the crooks got away. Outraged, Newell and a friend started a campaign for a statewide force, eventually writing two books and enlisting the aid of people such as Franklin Delano Roosevelt, then an obscure government official and hopeful politician.

It took until 1917 for Newell to convince the state legislature. The first superintendent of the force, a surgeon and ex-cavalryman named Dr. George Fletcher Chandler, was a controversial figure who immediately established the troopers as a force apart from others. He put them on horses and armed his officers with Colt .45 revolvers, holstered outside their coats in plain and intimidating view, a radical departure at the time. He established a mandatory police school, and insisted on an austere, army-like—some say quasi-religious—existence for his men. Their original headquarters buildings were known as barracks because they literally were. The troopers lived there year round.

Today, the force numbers about 4,000, organized into regional units known as troops. About 2,500 of its members are the familiar road troopers who wear gray uniforms and big cavalry hats; instead of charging around on horses, they command blue and gold cruisers. Approximately 1,000 other members of the agency are plainclothes detectives, members of the Bureau of Criminal Investigation, where they start as investigators and can work up to senior investigators, as well as through the command ranks. All of the BCI members started as regular troopers; to a man—and woman—they still talk about their early days on the road as "the good old days." Extensively trained, investigators tend to have a broad range of experience; they also tend to have some specialty beyond "mere" detective work as well. Plainclothes and uniformed members of the same troop often work together, and the force has an enviable *esprit de corps*. The department staffs three regional crime labs with state-of-the-art equipment, including a DNA facility.

Headquartered in Middletown, the exact center of Orange County, Troop F is responsible for several rural and suburban counties on the west side of the Hudson River. Its BCI unit handles maybe 12,000 cases a year, according to Nevins. Homicides aren't a big part of the total, with numbers running from twenty to thirty-five or so, depending on the year. But they're naturally among the most important cases the troop handles.

By the time Lieutenant Nevins got to the scene, a lot of the work had already been divvied up and was underway. Given that they already had a body, already had potential witnesses, might even already have potential suspects, the most important thing for the investigators to do was establish a timeline around the crime. It was a way of organizing what had happened, a powerful way of talking and thinking about it, a way that would make sense and show what gaps needed to be filled. It meant that working on the investigation was like trying to fill out a giant time chart, accounting for every minute, every second if possible, of the time around the crime. You didn't necessarily know what was important when you started, so you tried to get everything. "Timeline" was a mantra for Nevins and his men: Who did what, when, and where? Then what happened?

Other things were important as well, if a case was going to be made. The investigators were trained to look for subtle things that might demonstrate what Nevins called "clear-headedness," and what prosecutors could use at a trial to prove intent. Receipts of items used for the murder, for example, might be evidence of planning. Or, if they were for items purchased with money stolen during or after the crime, could show there hadn't been any remorse.

All of that translated into a mountain of grunt work, taxing even the state police's considerable manpower. Every member of the Saugerties police department except its chief was pressed into service, joining not just the routine traffic and security work but helping troopers with interviews of neighbors, store clerks, shop owners—anyone and everyone who might fill in the timeline. Though not unheard of, the cooperation with the local department was a point of honor for Nevins, who continually preached that his men ought to "throw their egos out the window" when working—not necessarily a line from Bartlet's Familiar Quotations, official police version.

While the troopers were getting their act together, they called the district attorney to let him know what was going on. Senior Investigator Dan Brown, another of the troop's trusted veterans, was slotted to handle the search warrants and the legal concerns.

As he got out of his car, Nevins spotted the two cars holding the suspects. Information started flying at him. Somewhere in his brain the fact that he might have juvenile suspects tripped a wire dictating an elaborate protocol. The script for dealing with youthful offenders can get pretty elaborate; parents or guardians must be present when they are questioned, for example, and they must be held separately from adult suspects. And then there's the human factor—talking to kids is always different than talking to adults.

Wendy Gardner and James Evans weren't suspects yet, not officially anyway. They were just two kids sitting in the back of patrol cars. Waiting.

Nevins went to find Collins. The bosses always tried to hold certain investigators back for certain jobs, slotting them into roles they were well suited for. He already had someone in mind for the interviews.

It turned out Eddie Collins was thinking the same way. Among the investigators en route to the scene was Stan O'Dell, a youthful-looking thirty-four-year-old bachelor with a round Irish face and greased-back hair straight out of the fifties. He'd first worked with Nevins back when he was a uniformed trooper across the river. Like a lot of the other guys called in that day, O'Dell had an impressive personnel folder. He'd been among the first troopers in the state to be trained in drug recognition—a protocol that allows police officers to diagnose what drugs a suspect is using without chemical tests. O'Dell had worked narcotics in New York City and was a member of the state police dive team. But what Nevins and Collins wanted him to do today was talk, and more importantly, listen. He was tagged to do the sit-downs with James Evans.

What made the investigator an effective interviewer wasn't his hail-fellow-well-met manner or even his well-schooled background. It was more his voice—so drop-dead calm and reassuring that other troopers called him "Father O'Dell." Have a conversation with him, and you'd swear he was the high school guidance counselor you always wished you had.

The match in personalities was something inspired—the volatile kid and the priest, a 1990s version of the Dead End Kids.

Except this wasn't a Saturday afternoon matinee.

Though assigned to a barracks in Greene County some miles away, O'Dell had lived in Saugerties for several years, and was well-known at the Exchange Hotel, a landmark workingman's bar and restaurant in the center of town. But he didn't know the Gardners, or James Evans.

When he got the call at the Catskill barracks, O'Dell had been given a minimum of information: "Put down the paperwork and meet me at Barclay Heights," Collins told him. Though the distance as the crow flies is only twelve miles or so, the winding roads and the mountains, as well as local traffic, can add considerable time to the drive; someone without a murder to get to can take a half hour or more.

O'Dell did it in about half that. He tried to clear his mind as he drove his Chevy Lumina south, slipping into automatic cop mode. Out of the car, he went up to Collins, who told him there had been a homicide and that he was to assist in the transport of two kids who had been in the house. They were being taken back to the Kingston barracks.

At the moment, no one—O'Dell especially—was precisely sure what they had, except for a dead body in the Mercury parked in the driveway. And the investigator had long ago learned not to ask the bosses any more questions than absolutely necessary at the scene.

Standard police procedure calls for potential witnesses to be kept separated for several reasons, most importantly so they don't "pollute" each other's stories. If the witnesses turn out to be suspects, of course, keeping them separate is even more critical.

Wendy Gardner and James Evans were sitting in separate cars, uncuffed since they were officially only people to be talked to. O'Dell slid behind the wheel of the car Wendy was in, noting only that she was quiet, and young. He checked in on the radio and glanced across at the town police car where James was. Everything ready, he slipped the transmission into drive and started out of the development.

They hadn't gotten very far when the town cop called over the radio for assistance. Evans was going ballistic in the backseat of his cruiser, screaming and yelling, threatening to kick out the windows.

"Stay right here a second," O'Dell told Gardner, pulling over. He jumped out of the car and hustled to the black and white. Evans was yelling about wanting his mother, about not wanting handcuffs, about not having done anything.

Leaning inside, O'Dell told James to calm down; he wasn't under arrest, and his mother would meet him at the station. He would not be handcuffed—at least not unless he was placed under arrest. He was a witness, not a suspect.

While not among some of the true giants who work for the state police, the investigator was taller than Evans and bulkier, and so had a certain physical intimidation factor working in his favor. But his main weapon was one of persuasion—the soft, calming voice of Father O'Dell telling Satch nothing was going to happen as long as he played it by the rules.

Whether it was the voice, the words, or O'Dell's size, Evans calmed down. The ride to the small Kingston barracks was quick and uneventful. Back in his car, O'Dell noted that Wendy was still sitting quietly in the back. If either wondered what the other was thinking, the questions went unasked.

14

"Someday I'll kill you"

Saturday, Dec. 31, 1994 Continued

Among the other investigators the bosses were holding out for the interviews was Kevin Costello, an eight-year veteran about as opposite from O'Dell as Sam Spade is from Hercule Poirot. Where O'Dell was polish and schmooze, Costello was street-smart, don't-bullshit-me business. He frowned where O'Dell smiled, and wore cynicism like a mismatched coat over a liberal cop's concern. His barrel-chest covered a big heart, but he didn't come off like a priest, Irish or otherwise; he shook his balding head too quickly, and his English was too damn plain.

One thing he and O'Dell had in common, though—they did good interviews.

Costello had run up to the scene and gotten the same routine O'Dell had. Told to transport Kathy Gardner down to the Kingston barracks in a marked trooper car, he did the job with quick dispatch. Though referred to as Kingston, the barracks are actually located a short distance outside the city proper in a very rural town called Hurley; in fact, the barracks amount to the center of town, sitting across from a small Stewart's and down the hill from an old church. A state highway runs nearby and the road affords quick access to the Thruway as well as east-west connectors. From the front, the barracks look like a plain residential ranch-style house. However, from around the side, it's clear there are a few more offices there than a typical residential unit would have. Barracks such as these, with dark paneling and well-scuffed floors—not to mention plumbing that sometimes backs up and air conditioning units older than the trooper manning the front desk—are common throughout the state. Desks are jammed into small rooms, and computers are situated anywhere they'll fit are the norm.

Costello led Kathy Gardner inside to the BCI squad room at the end of the hallway in the front part of the building. Barely big enough for its four desks, the room had a few homey touches that humanized the clutter: posters, a coffee machine, an inexpensive microwave. Kathy sat down in the corner while Costello went to consult with the bosses, find out what the next step was. The place was rapidly becoming crowded; within hours, Senior Investigator Collins' small office would be overrun with other seniors and the lieutenant, who constantly traded information and advice as they pulled the case together.

Costello admired Collins a lot. To an outsider, the senior investigator could come off a bit gruff, even crusty, but he lived and breathed police work, could make snap judgments that stuck, and on pure, old-fashioned gumshoe stuff there might not have been a better cop in the whole troop. Collins told Costello he was going to talk to Kathy. It was, in a sense, the most important interview of the case, for already the bosses had a feeling that the whole story was going to flow from the eleven-year-old's mouth. Building a case from interviews is a step-by-step procedure, knowledge building upon knowledge, and what the little girl with her troubled expression told Costello would be critical for the other interviews.

If it went right.

Costello walked back into the squad room and sat down with Kathy. Closing the door, the room suddenly seemed to dwarf them. Almost from the moment she opened her mouth, the thirty-seven-year-old investigator was struck by the eleven-year-old's articulateness. She had a strong sense of right and wrong; what she had seen was wrong, and she wanted the police to know all about it. With some gentle prodding from Costello, her story worked itself into chronological order.

"During the past year," she started, "my grandmother and my sister have not been getting along very well." They were yelling and screaming and fighting all the time. "Sometime after the summer, my sister was fighting with my grandmother, and my sister slapped my grandmother."

Kathy Gardner went on to describe another time when the two were fighting. Her sister had screamed, "Someday I'll kill you."

Costello nodded, listening. He tended not to ask too many questions as long as the girl kept talking. It was his style, a style he was used to, and the reason he was in the room in the first place.

"Wendy and James were always together, and rarely hung out with the rest of us," Kathy said. "Most of the time, Wendy and James were by themselves, and Wendy told me that they were having sexual intercourse on a regular basis. In October, just before her birthday, Wendy ran away from home, and told us she was far away, but the police found her staying at the Evans residence in Saugerties."

In order for police to take formal statements and confessions admissible in New York State's courts from youthful suspects, their parents must be present. Dinah Evans had been located almost immediately near the house. In fact, she had at first thought her son was dead, and was near hysteria before being reassured by her daughter that he wasn't. The two women quickly headed to the station. Clarence "Buzz" Gardner, Wendy and Kathy's father, however, lived some towns away, down in the New Paltz area.

His notification and arrival at the station would later end up being somewhat controversial. Several troopers said they had difficulty locating him at first, and that a detail was sent specifically to locate him. Another source said he was notified at home by someone other than the police and came down immediately. When he arrived, troopers and other witnesses say, he complained loudly that the system had screwed up, and had to be calmed by the investigators, including Collins himself.

Buzz Gardner, on the other hand, told others later that he arrived promptly and was kept from speaking to his daughters, Wendy in particular. There appears to have also been some legitimate confusion about his proper legal status. While he was the girls' natural father, their legal guardian was his mother Betty, who at the moment was waiting for the coroner to arrive back in Saugerties.

In any event, Buzz Gardner was present when Costello began the interview that became Kathy's deposition, and signed the document along with her. According to the investigator, he did not interfere with the interviews and sat listening with a combination of concern and shock on his face. The legality of the girl's statement was not challenged in the pre-trial hearings.

Investigator Costello kept taking notes as the young girl talked. A former air force security officer who'd been in the BCI for about three years, Costello had heard and seen a lot of stories before. He wasn't particularly surprised by this one, even though it was different than any other case he'd handled. What got him were the details the kid gave him, stuff that kept coming back, things it was impossible to make up. No way she was lying, he thought. She really had her stuff together.

They went through the events of the last three days several times, pausing for breaks here and there. Costello would occasionally go outside to one of the offices where the other investigators were, keeping tabs on what else was going on, getting and feeding information back and forth.

"I was in the kitchen watching the little TV, and my grandmother was in the family room in the basement watching the large TV," Kathy Gardner told the investigator, recalling the night of the murder. "I heard someone open the front door, and Wendy came into the kitchen. Wendy asked me to come downstairs, but I refused. I walked into the living room, and I observed that James Evans was standing on the stair landing, next to the front door. Wendy put her bag down, and asked me to go downstairs with her a second time. I didn't want to, but I did anyway. James, Wendy, and myself walked down the stairs, into the basement family room, where my grandmother was watching TV."

She started talking a little faster, making it hard for Costello to keep up with his notes.

"James says to Wendy, 'Say what you have to say.' But Wendy replied, 'No, just do it.' My grandmother then said to James, 'What are you doing? This is my house, please get out.' "

Kathy paused before going on.

"James says to her, 'No.' My grandmother then started to walk around him, and James put both hands on her chest, and pushed her back."

Costello and Buzz Gardner listened as the eleven-year-old recounted the fight, recalled being dragged toward the stairs, told of seeing her grandmother's legs buckle. "She fell down to her knees," recalled Kathy. "James still did not let go. He kept his grip on her neck."

The words came out flat and even, pouring with the gush of someone who had seen something horrible and wanted it out, wanted it all recorded. She told how Evans and her sister had discussed what to do with the body. She told how she had been kept prisoner for the next two days, how she had debated what to do, and then how she had finally escaped and run away to the neighbors' house. She talked and talked, adding detail to detail with a vivid account of all she had seen.

With most of the story out, Costello began asking specific questions. His job now was to rule out others' alibis and zero in on the most incriminating facts. He was like an artist, filling in a few final details in a broadly sketched painting.

"Did Wendy kick your grandmother when she was being killed or after she was dead?" he asked.

"No."

"Was Andy Bender in the house when your grandmother was killed?"

"No."

"Where did you get the scratches on your face?"

"From Wendy when we were fighting, while James choked my grandmother."

Finally finished with the statement, Costello looked up at the clock on the wall. It was now just after 9:30 P.M. They had begun talking together a few minutes before three, six-and-a-half hours ago.

His plans for New Year's Eve and his girlfriend's birthday were all shot to hell, but the trooper didn't think about that at all. Instead, he took one last look at the little girl who'd just finished talking to him. He'd come to like her a lot, even admire her, over these past hours.

As he left the room, Costello thought to himself that she had been dealt a rotten hand and done her best with it. Maybe God would take care of her, he thought; she sure as hell had it coming.

15

Face

Dinah Evans knew something was going on as soon as she saw the police cars at the end of the block. A knot of neighbors had gathered on one of the lawns between her house and Betty Gardner's. She walked toward them at something more than a deliberate pace, her instincts tingling.

Then someone told her James was dead and she went crazy, running toward the police cars like an avenging demon.

Her daughter Donna finally grabbed her and told her James was sitting in the police car. The world began passing in a daze, events sliding around as if seen from a carnival carousel. Informed that Betty was dead and that James had to be questioned, the two women headed down to the barracks, trying to make sense from insanity.

Dinah didn't like Stan O'Dell. He struck her as a phony, and she wasn't the kind of person to keep her opinions to herself. She asked to call the attorney who had been assigned as James' legal advisor during the family court proceedings. It was New Year's Eve, though, and he apparently wasn't home. In the meantime, advised of his rights, James Evans began answering questions on his own.

The first thing O'Dell realized when he walked into the interview room with investigator Wayne Olsen to begin speaking to Evans was that he wasn't talking to a "normal" fifteen-year-old. Most fifteen-year-olds, in O'Dell's experience, were scared to death about dealing with the police. James Evans had wise-guy oozing from every pore. He seemed to know how to handle himself, and in O'Dell's estimation, knew how to twist a few real facts around a falsehood.

But "Father" O'Dell was patient. The first thing Evans said was that he didn't know how Betty Gardner had been killed.

It would have been obvious to anyone, much less an experienced police investigator, that the kid wasn't telling the whole story. But O'Dell and the other investigators let him tell the story his way, letting him lay out the vast gaps.

Then they started asking questions, simple ones, almost dumb ones. When it was obvious that the I-know-nothing slant wasn't playing, Evans changed his story. He implicated a friend in a Camaro. This sounded more plausible, like there might be a little bit of truth here at least. O'Dell drew out details slowly, realizing it was another fabrication.

His round face appeared unruffled, but inside the investigator was struggling to keep focused. James Evans was difficult to talk to. If you pushed too hard, he quickly became agitated, volatile. Several times, he seemed ready to punch someone, and O'Dell was the most likely candidate. The teenager slid his chair back to the edge of the wall in the small room, as if challenging him to make the first move.

Father O'Dell schmoozed, soothed, coaxed him back.

"No one's ever going to put handcuffs on me," said James.

O'Dell explained again that witnesses were never handcuffed. You only got handcuffed if you were a suspect charged with a crime. It was a deft dodge. As the day dragged on it was becoming clearer and clearer that James Evans was intimately involved in the murder, but O'Dell's explanation calmed him down.

What was James Evans thinking? He'd dealt with police before for minor scrapes, and had a long history of interviews with family court judges, parole officers, and town police. Maybe he figured he could bluff his way through once more, or maybe he told himself this was going to be just one more time like all the rest— worst case, society would slap him on the wrist. Maybe he thought he was fried no matter what he said. Maybe he was just a tough guy with a rotten attitude, somebody who figured the whole rest of the world could go to hell.

Or maybe he was a fifteen-year-old in so deep all he could see was ocean.

He had never been in anywhere near such serious trouble before, and for all his tough-guy image, he was naive about a lot of things. The state troopers were about the last people in the world who would back down or be impressed if he started smashing things. And if he thought he could outsmart them, he was badly mistaken. He'd been told he had the right to remain silent, and have a lawyer present, yet he went ahead and answered questions—slowly, reluctantly, but still, there it was. Anything he said sure as hell wouldn't help him.

In the rap songs he'd listened to for the past few days, the murderers were smart guys who came out ahead even when they went down. Face was the important thing. Jail, the streets—it was more or less the same thing, one seamless world. You kept your cynical, shotgun-toting attitude cooking as long as you could breathe.

Gradually, like fishermen working a recalcitrant trout stream, Stan O'Dell and Wayne Olsen worked around to something approximating the true story. They went over it, for the record.

"Do you understand your rights as I have read them to you," O'Dell asked.

"Yeah," Evans answered.

"Do you know why you are here today?"

"Because Wendy's grandmother is dead."

O'Dell nodded. "Do you know how she died?"

"Yes. Sort of."

"Can you tell me?"

"She was strangled."

"James, do you know who strangled her?" the investigator asked.

"I think I did."

Father O'Dell was in high gear now, not even pausing to catch his breath. "Can you tell me how it happened?"

Evans claimed that on the day of the murder, he had been playing pool in a local billiards hall, met a friend and driven up to Palenville where he got drunk on vodka screwdrivers and Kahlua. Perhaps it was a coincidence, but the story he told bore at least a passing resemblance to one of the scenarios on Snoop Doggy Dogg's *Doggystyle* tape. It left out Wendy completely, placing her at her house when James was dropped off there by a friend sometime after 10:30 P.M.

"What happened when you got to Wendy's?" O'Dell asked.

"She let me in and that's all I remember."

"James, you told me that you thought you strangled Wendy's grandmother. Why do you think you strangled her?"

"When I woke up Thursday morning I had cord marks around my fingers on my right hand and I had a flashback of me on Wendy's grandmother's back, and I had a left hand on her back and was pulling on a cord that was around her neck with my right hand."

O'Dell continued in his calm, confessional voice. "Do you remember where the cord came from, or what you did with it?"

"I don't know. It might still be on her. I don't know where it came from."

"Is there any reason why you would be fighting with Wendy's grandmother?"

"No, not unless she was fighting with Wendy. I might have grabbed her."

"What happened to Wendy's grandmother after she was strangled?"

"She got put in the trunk."

O'Dell nodded. "Who put her in the trunk?"

"I don't remember." Evans flared. "I was too drunk. I don't know if I did, Wendy or Kathy did."

O'Dell seemed to back off a bit, but in reality he was nailing James to the wall. "Was there anyone else at the house besides Wendy, Kathy, and yourself?"

"No, not that night."

"Did you take any money from Wendy's grandmother?"

"Yes."

By Evans' count, they had taken somewhere between $750 and $830 from Mrs. Gardner the night she was killed. He told how they had spent much of it at the mall, and on gas and food. He also said he had given his friends Andy Bender $25 and Barry Green $5.

"How did you get around?" O'Dell asked.

"I drove Wendy's grandmother's car," answered the fifteen-year-old.

"Where was Wendy's grandmother's body when you were driving around?"

"In the trunk."

The questions were tight now, very directed, even if O'Dell's manner made it look like he was just shooting the breeze. Every word that James Evans said about the body was one more nail in the box the state police were constructing around him. Even the lies were incriminating.

"What were you going to do with the body?" O'Dell asked.

"We didn't know. The only two ideas were to put it up in a burned-out schoolhouse in Palenville, or we were going to burn it in her house."

"Who knew what happened to Wendy's grandmother?"

"Kathy, Wendy, Andy, and me."

"How did the others know about it?"

"Kathy and Wendy Gardner were there when it happened, and Kathy told Andy about it."

"Did you tell any of the others not to tell anyone about what happened?"

"I think Kathy was told not to tell anyone."

"Do you remember Kathy or Wendy fighting with their grandmother or having any physical contact with her?"

"No."

O'Dell continued on, asking questions about a phone, switching to the bag that had been thrown into the dumpster, then coming back to the body in the back of the car. The way he put it, everything seemed innocuous, a winding conversation that just happened to be about murder. "When the body was put into the trunk of the car, where was the car?"

"In the garage," James answered. "The garage door was down and the car was driven in."

"Do you remember who put the body in the trunk?"

"Me and Wendy."

O'Dell scribbled the conversation down on a lined statement sheet, writing as quickly as he could. James Evans and his mother signed the top portion, indicating that they had been advised of their rights. But James refused to answer O'Dell when he asked if he knew that making a false written statement was a crime, and then balked at signing the statement summarizing their interview as O'Dell wrote it.

He seems to have thought that by not signing the document, his statement could not be used against him.

But under New York's rules of evidence, the investigator was free to tell a jury everything James had told him.

One of the investigators told Evans that he needed the Dallas Cowboys' jersey he was wearing. James took it off, then started to get upset.

"Hey, where are you going with my clothes?" he demanded as the shirt was taken away. "I bought those."

"You bought those with the money you stole," O'Dell told him.

"But they're mine."

O'Dell walked away, shaking his head. The kid just didn't get it.

16

A cold, exact voice

Saturday, Dec. 31, 1994 Continued

It was late by the time the investigators were ready to talk to Wendy Gardner. Wives or girlfriends had been called hours ago, New Year's Eve plans canceled. Most of the women understood; canceled plans came with their loved ones' jobs.

By now, the investigators had a fairly good idea of what had happened. Besides the interviews with Kathy Gardner and James Evans, the bosses were putting together information from other witnesses, including Andy Bender, Barry Green, the neighbors, and a myriad of others. There was also physical evidence: the rug recovered from the dumpster, receipts of the teenagers' shopping spree, a blood-stained glove, a hundred-dollar bill found on the kitchen table, video games, tapes, a collection of pennies—all the trivial paraphernalia of a murder scene.

And there was the body itself. Stuffed face-down into the trunk, dressed in plaid pants and a sweatshirt, the corpse bore the plain costume of a woman who'd struggled to make ends meet, who spent more on her grandchildren than on herself.

Nevins' timeline was rapidly filling in. To be sure, there were some gaps left, and different variations of the stories to check out. Had Evans really been drunk? Where had the murder weapon come from? Had robbery been a motive?

But the BCI investigators had it, more or less. They knew that Evans and Gardner had come by Wednesday night, that Evans had strangled the old woman downstairs while Gardner held her sister, that the teenagers had spent the next two days partying and riding around with grandma's body in the back of the trunk.

What they didn't have was an answer to a more nagging, more difficult question, the sort of thing that can't be filled in by blood samples or shoe prints.

Why did Betty Gardner have to die?

Kathy Gardner had given them some information, and Dinah Evans was already talking about abuse, but none of it seemed to be enough. Maybe it was the money, some of the investigators thought. To these kids—to most kids—eight or nine hundred bucks was a lot of walking-around money.

Maybe James Evans was just a homicidal maniac, others held; he'd already tried to kick out the back of a police car, after all.

If anybody knew, it was Wendy Gardner. As the last hour of 1994 began, Investigators Kevin Costello and

Stan O'Dell headed into the interrogation room with Wendy's father to find out.

Wendy agreed to allow them to tape the interview. Ironically, neither investigator particularly liked using a tape recorder. O'Dell in particular felt that tape recordings tended to make it very easy to take things out of context. But this tape would prove to have considerable more context than any transcript.

As he activated the tape player and started to speak, Costello's voice broke. He sounded nervous, though he later denied he was nervous or anything at all.

"December 31, 1994, the time is 11:07 P.M.," he said, noting that Wendy and her father Buzz were present, and that she had been advised of her rights.

Suddenly, Buzz started to leave.

"We need you to stay," Costello told him.

"You're leaving?" Wendy asked plaintively.

"No, he's not going to leave, we need him to stay," Costello told her. "I need both of you to pay attention to me, OK? You have a right to remain silent. Anything you say can and will be used against you in the court of law."

He tripped over the standard Miranda warning, reread it. Buzz Gardner, meanwhile, sat back in the seat, silent. He seemed drained, more tired than anyone else in the room. His mother was dead and it was already obvious that his daughter was going to be charged with the crime.

No father could want to believe something like that. Buzz had never really gotten along with his parents, but this . . . .

"All right, having these rights in mind, do you wish to talk to me now?" Costello asked.

"Yes," said Wendy Gardner.

"Do you understand these rights?" the investigator asked Buzz.

He nodded.

"Say it verbally, please."

"Yes," answered Buzz, adding that Wendy had been arrested and charged.

"No," Costello said. "Right now, she's being interviewed relative to the homicide of her grandmother. In all probability, if she has [been] involved, she will be arrested."

Buzz Gardner started to ask if Costello thought there would be a charge, but his words fell off.

"Nothing's been promised to you today, correct?" Costello asked.

"Yes."

"And you haven't been given any special promise that we're going to do anything for you," Costello continued. "The only thing we're telling you, that we're asking for the truth. Do you understand that?"

"Yes," said Wendy. Her face was puffy from fatigue, though she was probably more used to late hours than the investigators at the table with her.

"OK," said Costello. "So why don't you go ahead and explain to us exactly what, uh, happened, uh, during the course of the past week between you, James Evans, and your grandmother in Saugerties."

Wendy Gardner nodded. "OK."

"Right from the beginning," put in O'Dell.

"All the way?"

"Yep," said Costello.

In a cold voice that could have been reading from a prepared script, Wendy Gardner began to tell her story. It came out in full sentences and paragraphs, perfectly punctuated, laid out with no prodding from either investigator. It came out complete with sound effects and different inflections for each person she talked about, including herself.

"Christmas night," she began, "after we opened all our presents, me, I was sitting on James' lap and I wanted to stay there for Christmas, and he said . . . because it's Christmas, why don't you call? Because I had been put on PINS petition and I wasn't allowed to even be over there. So I called and asked if I could stay there for the night and she automatically said no."

"This being your grandmother," offered Costello.

"Yes."

"OK."

"She said no, I don't want you being there at all," continued Wendy. "You're never gonna go back there again. And I said in my own words, fuck you bitch. I'm staying here tonight no matter what you say. After that I hung up and I talked to James a little bit. I said, she's such a bitch over and over again. Then I called her a second time to ask her and then I hung up and I called her again and the phone kept ringing and ringing and ringing and she didn't answer. And then I called another time and this time she said if you keep calling, I'm going to call the police. So that put me into a rage and I got up and talked to James some more and I said, I want to kill her so bad."

Costello and O'Dell sat back and listened as Wendy Gardner recounted in her cold, exact voice precisely how she and James Evans had spent the next few days walking around the neighborhood plotting the killing. The two investigators had planned to work off each other. Although there was no set script, in general one would establish the facts and the other would come in with specific questions to nail down inconsistencies or gaps. But there was no need for strategy now; for much of the time they just sat back and listened, trying not to betray surprise or emotion—not about the details of the murder, many of which they knew already, but about the girl's methodical and seemingly remorseless manner.

". . . We stopped right at the end of Rose Lane on the road close to where I live, and right in the middle to where he lives, and again he asked me if we're gonna do it, and I said. 'Yes, I want it done. We plan too much. I want it over with.' He said OK," Gardner recalled, recounting how they came into the house and told Kathy to come downstairs with them. "I walked over to the TV and shut off the TV, hit the knob and, um, my grandmother goes, 'Wendy, what's going on here?' And James goes, 'Go ahead, tell her what you're going to tell her.' I remember what I said I was going to tell her now when we're talking. 'You beat me. Now we're gonna—' "

"Did you tell her that?" Costello asked.

"No. 'Cause they got into a fight before I could. 'You beat me then, now it's your turn to get beaten.' We were gonna beat her first."

"But you didn't do that."

"No."

"All right. Just tell us what happened."

"Um, James said, 'Go ahead, say something.' And I go, 'What?' Cause I was so upset and thought that he was just gonna jump on her and kill her but he didn't, and then I forgot about the plan pretty much and he says, 'Come on, we're gonna do what the plan says, right?' And then my grandma says, 'Wendy, what's going on here?' And James goes, 'Shut up, it's none of your business,' and then she got up and said, 'You shut up.

You're in my house, just get out, now.' And then James goes, 'Bitch. Get out of my face.' So they're pushing each other and my sister goes, 'Wendy, stop that. James, come on.' And then I go, 'Shut up, Kathy. You don't know what he's gonna do. You don't know what he's gonna do.' And then we were talking more, me and my sister, and I go, 'Better be quiet.' And she goes, 'Why? Why? What's going to happen?' And all of a sudden I see James lunge at my grandmother 'cause she was backing away, lunge at her and she had a glass of water and they spun around and her water glass went around and spun the water all over the couch and on the table and my grandmother was struggling for a while and Kathy was screaming so loud and I said, 'Be quiet, be quiet, he's gonna kill her. I don't want him to kill you too, 'cause if the police come he'll kill you.' So she started to quiet down. Then she screamed more so I, um, slapped her in the face, kicked her and smashed her head into the wall . . .''

Wendy Gardner continued with hardly an interruption, calmly reciting the details, occasionally taking on other parts in the macabre play of death she and Evans had just lived out. She mimicked the sound of the body hitting the floor. "Thud." She replayed Grandma being dragged from the basement to the garage. "Shhhhh, thud, cur-shh.''

Side A of the tape ran out. Costello scrambled to spin it around. O'Dell just tried to take it all in and keep his eyes from popping.

The tape rolled again and the story went on. The bells of the church up the hill began to toll. It was 1995.

As she continued, Wendy Gardner grew more and more tired. She became confused about what they had done on what day; details began blurring together. But the whole time her tone remained cold, matter-of-fact; she could have been recalling a family vacation.

All of a sudden it hit O'Dell—the grandmother died because the two kids wanted to have sex and she wouldn't let them.

Grandma was a bitch, and she had to die.

Jesus.

He put his priest's voice back on, trying to straighten out the timeline. He asked Wendy Gardner about what they had done Friday, two days after the murder.

"We went back to McDonald's 'cause we wanted some fries," she told him. Then they had driven over to the bowling alley, then back. O'Dell asked what they had done after they had gone inside McDonald's and Wendy corrected him, saying that they hadn't gone inside.

"We didn't. We didn't go in and eat at McDonald's because Kathy was screaming that she didn't want to wait out in the car again," she told him.

"OK."

"So James goes, 'Fuck it, why don't we just go to the mall.' And I said, 'You're gonna go through Kingston? And he goes, yeah.'"

"OK, so that's when you went to the mall and you bought those things? So after the mall, you went back to the house. Did you go anyplace Friday night? Or was that the night you stayed home and fell asleep, you said."

"That's the night when we got home, James fell asleep on the couch, then I fell asleep and Kathy fell asleep."

"OK. And then, Saturday morning when you woke up, that's when the police were there."

"Yes."

"How did the police get there?" asked Buzz Gardner making his first comment since the interview began more than an hour earlier. "I still don't understand."

"I know," agreed Wendy. "That's what I don't understand."

"Where did the police come from?" Buzz demanded.

O'Dell didn't answer—directly. "Where was your sister Saturday morning?" he asked instead.

"I don't know."

"All right. Do you have anything else you'd like to add to this statement?"

"Um, it doesn't help now, but I wish it didn't happen."

Elizabeth "Betty" Gardner. (*Photo courtesy Ulster County, N.Y. District Attorney's Office*)

Betty Gardner opening Christmas presents at her home in happier times. (*Photo courtesy Ulster County, N.Y. District Attorney's Office*)

The Gardner home in Barclay Heights, Saugerties, N.Y. on December 31, 1994, the day the murder was discovered.
(*Photo courtesy New York State Police*)

State troopers photographed Wendy Gardner, 13, on the day of her interview to document that she had not been mistreated during questioning.
(*Photo courtesy New York State Police*)

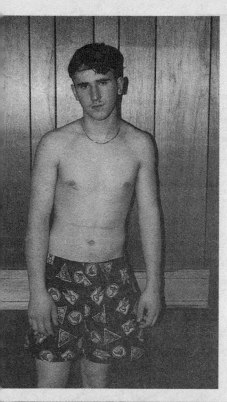

James Evans, 15, was also photographed on December 31, 1994, the day the teenagers were questioned. (*Photo courtesy New York State Police*)

Betty Gardner's body was found in the trunk of her 1984 Mercury. (*Photo courtesy New York State Police*)

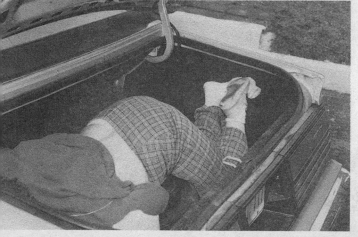

A piece of nylon-reinforced kite string was used by Evans to strangle Betty Gardner.

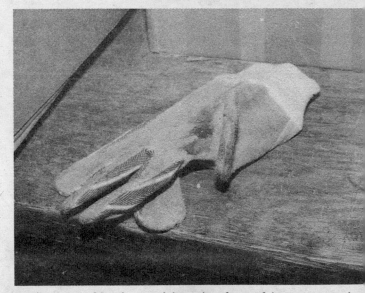

The victim's blood stained the palm of one of the canvas work gloves Evans wore during the murder.

Wendy Gardner wrote about her volatile relationships in her diary.

A sole one hundred dollar bill was all that remained of Betty Gardner's money after the teenagers' partying and shopping spree.

The basement rec room where Betty Gardner was murdered before it was examined by state troopers. James Evans and Wendy Gardner removed the blood-stained carpet and then folded out the couch to have sex. (*Photo courtesy New York State Police*)

Betty Gardner was buried next to her husband Clarence in the St. Mary of the Snow Cemetery in Saugerties, N.Y., less than a ten-minute walk from the Gardner home.

Holding a teddy bear, Wendy Gardner leaves Saugerties town court on January 5, 1995. (*Photo courtesy* Kingston Daily & Sunday Freeman; *photo by Bill Madden*)

Wendy Gardner being led to her arraignment on charges that she murdered her grandmother. (*Photo courtesy* Kingston Daily & Sunday Freeman)

James Evans remained in the custody of the state after being indicted by the grand jury for the murder of Elizabeth Gardner. (*Photo courtesy* Kingston Daily & Sunday Freeman)

Clarence "Buzz" Gardner, Jr., the victim's son, being sworn in at the trial of his daughter Wendy. (*Photo courtesy* Kingston Daily & Sunday Freeman)

Investigator Stan O'Dell was one of the state troopers who interviewed James Evans.

BCI Investigator Kevin Costello's interview with Wendy Gardner's sister Kathy would prove critical to the prosecution's case against the teenagers.

Ulster County, N.Y. Court Judge J. Michael Bruhn presided at both trials.

Dan Gaffney of the Ulster County, N.Y. Public Defender's Office served as counsel for James Evans.

Wendy Gardner was represented at her trial by Jeremiah "Jerry" Flaherty, one of Ulster County, N.Y.'s top criminal defense lawyers.

Mike Kavanaugh, Ulster County, N.Y. District Attorney, saw to a swift indictment for the teenagers before turning the case over to an assistant D.A.

Ulster County, N.Y. Assistant District Attorney Michael Miranda prosecuted both cases.

17

Brain dump

Sunday, Jan. 1, 1995

They'd called him earlier in the day, so Saugerties
Town Judge David Wachtel knew more or less what to
expect. Still, entering the town offices and the small
courtroom, he felt a chill sweep through him. He lived
in Simmons Park, not far from the murder scene. He
had known Betty Gardner. As a matter of fact, he'd said
hello to her in the supermarket just a few days ago. He
knew she'd been trying to take care of the kids, knew
she'd had a lot of trouble with their father. James Evans
he didn't know, but Dinah had been before him for
petty crimes; he'd put her on probation.

Wachtel had been a trooper himself for twenty-two
years, pulling his own stint in the BCI. In New York
State, town judges don't have to be lawyers; the local
bench has a long tradition of lay judges who are thor-

oughly familiar with the laws that pertain to their courts and are able to mix a high degree of common sense with legal knowledge. Wachtel in particular was a realist. He once told a visitor on court night that, if he doffed his robes, he could walk outside and buy dope in five minutes. The people who came before him tended to fall into predictable patterns: there were the traffic tickets, of course, and then there were the kids who'd done something dumb and wouldn't be back. There were also the kids who sat in the back of the room telling jokes while working their way toward bigger and better crimes. Finally, there were the habitual petty criminals, who came decked out in the sheriff's orange overalls, legs chained together, stopping off in Wachtel's court like some tourists on a world cruise—Saugerties tonight, Woodstock tomorrow, Kingston Friday. But this case was in a category of its own.

In upstate New York, criminal charges in a serious case are generally first presented in a local court in a formal process known as an arraignment. From there, felony murder cases usually are brought to a grand jury, which determines whether there is sufficient evidence for an indictment and trial. While preliminary hearings can occasionally take place in a local court, most proceedings in felony cases generally take place in county courts, where there are more facilities and resources.

Wachtel's role, therefore, was limited. His job tonight was essentially to look over the charges the state police made and make sure there was enough evidence to start the process. He wasn't judging anyone guilty of anything; if anything, he was making sure the potential defendants were not being railroaded.

He also had to consider what to do with them. In theory, the judge could have set bail or even released them to their parents, but it was clear those weren't serious options. Typically, murder suspects in Ulster County spend all of their time before trial in jail.

But the age of the suspects complicated matters somewhat. James Evans was fifteen, some weeks shy of his sixteenth birthday. Wendy Gardner was thirteen. Under New York State law, they could be tried as adults for murder, but they could not be sentenced as adults. Nor could minors before trial be kept with adult suspects until they turned at least sixteen.

The state troopers brought the teenagers in to be arraigned. Outside in the hall, Evans and Gardner waved and smiled at each other, flashed signs. Investigator Costello, among the detail escorting them in, was amazed. Wendy had shown no remorse, nothing beyond feeling sorry for herself that she was in trouble.

They quieted as they were led inside. James hung back a little, talking to his mother. Wendy had her head down. It was all starting to sink in, maybe.

Wachtel slid back in his chair. His focus shifted for a second, blurring just a bit with the hour; it was well after two in the morning of a new day, a new year. The sixty-two-year-old judge ruminated briefly about his own kids and their young children, his grandchildren.

There was nothing you could do, really. Case like this. Grandmother had a hell of a job trying to raise those girls.

But geez. These kids were so young.

The papers were in order. The state troopers had more than enough evidence to make their arrest, to bring charges.

The judge pounded his gavel. He remanded both suspects to the custody of the sheriff, directing that they be placed in appropriate youth facilities. Having heard that they had mentioned suicide, he ordered them placed on suicide watch. He later would direct one of his clerks to make sure the order was followed through, an extra token of concern.

Ulster County does not have separate jail facilities for youthful detainees. The closest facility turned out to be on Long Island, over a hundred miles away. Arrangements made, the two murder suspects were whisked off into the night.

David Wachtel sighed, turned off the lights, and went home to his wife.

Back at the trooper barracks, Stan O'Dell found an empty desk and sat down. His mind went completely blank as he stared at the wall.

He called the fog a "brain dump," a short circuiting after everything that had happened, everything he'd heard.

Just blanking.

Finally he pulled himself together and went to write his report.

V

PRESUMED INNOCENT

18

Charged with murder

Monday, Jan. 2, 1995

Sometime early Monday morning, there was a knock on the door of Jeremiah Flaherty's home in rural Ulster County. Tucked into the far side of the Shawangunk Mountains, the house was a long way from the hard-boiled streets of the West Side of Manhattan, where a youthful Flaherty had lost his girlfriend to his cousin, who just happened to be the leader of the Westies, a notorious Irish-American street gang. The short, pugnacious kid with a quick temper but a faster mouth had turned a way with words and numbers into a razor-edged law practice. Like thousands of others, he'd fled the city to raise a family in the bucolic reaches of the Hudson Valley, a place known to any denizen of Manhattan's West Side only as "upstate." Now a sharp-dressing middle-aged man with a boxer's body and a splash of red in his white mustache and well-coifed hair, Flaherty had escaped the boiling cauldron he'd grown up in, but he carried bits of it around with him every day, in his walk, in his talk, and most especially in what he did. For the former West Side urchin was now one of the top criminal defense attorneys in the rural county, a guy who could juggle a half-dozen murder cases at any given moment and still find time to run down to town court and beat somebody's drug rap. Given to wearing light-colored suits that made him stand out in court, he was a familiar sight in several county courts, where he was often found chatting not just with other lawyers, but with defendants, clients, and non-clients alike.

But he did not like them knocking on his door, most especially on his day off. And though the man he found there was someone he had had the honor of representing before, he did not welcome Buzz Gardner in for coffee and cake.

Flaherty saw right away Gardner was there on something beyond his usual drug-related gig. Distraught and desperate, Wendy's father began telling him a story that even an attorney might find unbelievable.

His daughter had been charged with murdering his mother, Gardner said. Flaherty had to help her.

If the lawyer wasn't fully awake when he opened the door, he was now. Flaherty told Gardner not to worry, to call the office tomorrow—when it was open—and that he'd take the case.

It wasn't going to be charity. Gardner stood to inherit his mother's estate. Eventually, proceeds from the sale of Betty Gardner's house would go to pay for her murderer's defense.

* * *

James Evans had no such windfall working in his favor. His defense would be provided entirely by the public defender's office. In Ulster County, like many of the state's smaller communities, the word "office" is something of a misnomer; local attorneys are assigned different cases to handle along with their own private practices. Senior attorneys in Ulster tend to get the more important cases on an informal rotating basis. This one would fall to Dan Gaffney, a gray-haired, dapper Kingston lawyer with a brisk but friendly manner and a modest office in a tiny old house across from the courthouse parking lot.

Though he had considerable experience in criminal law, most of Gaffney's regular caseload involved personal injury lawsuits. His father, Charles H. Gaffney, was a legendary personal injury attorney in town. Dan followed in his footsteps in the mid-seventies, eventually "inheriting" the specialty. But the younger Gaffney developed his own reputation during his first days in practice by successfully mounting a self-defense argument in a murder case and he'd handled serious criminal cases ever since. He also had known the head of the public defender's office, Paul Gruner, since second grade. If there was an old-boy network among local lawyers, he was one of its charter members; even the district attorney spoke well of him.

There were some whispers around town that the tall man with the well-lined face had lost a few steps over the years, but most prosecutors seemed to count him as a formidable, knowledgeable opponent, a guy you took lightly at your case's peril. Up close, his ruggedly handsome face proved to be pockmarked, as if he were a fighter who put his chin out as a decoy, only to waste the sucker who dropped his guard in close. As a public defender, Gaffney often took cases with little hope. Still, he didn't like to lose, no matter what the odds were.

19

Why?

Monday, Jan. 2, 1995 Continued

"Teens held for killing grandma" screamed the banner headline on the *Kingston Daily Freeman* Monday morning. "Teens held in slaying," declared the rival *Times Herald Record*.

With most of their information based on a press conference held by the police and Ulster County District Attorney Michael Kavanagh on New Year's Day, the first stories laid out the bare facts of the case, lining them up more or less in the direction of the DA's case. Wendy Gardner and James Evans' ages played prominently. So did the preliminary cause of death—strangulation—and the fact that the teenagers had driven around for two days with Grandma in the trunk.

"It's very disturbing to me," Kavanagh declared. "It

should be disturbing to all of us that children in this community could be capable of such depravity.''

Kavanagh's reaction was echoed not only in comments by the neighbors, but by the community in general. For most people in Ulster County—for most people in America—the image of a kindly old grandmother being done in by two teenagers had an emotional impact far beyond the usual murder. And that was the way the papers and other media played it.

Though largely rural and without a sprawling metropolis, Kingston, the county seat, has a population under 25,000. Ulster did have its occasional homicide, even of the gruesome and senseless variety. After all, Dutch Schultz had roamed these hills during the Prohibition; part of his wealth was still rumored to be buried here. A grand jury had just indicted a man in a killing during a Chinese gang war. Though the murder had occurred elsewhere, Ulster was where the body was found. A spurned lover in Kingston decided to get revenge by killing a little girl and was soon discovered to have murdered before. Then there were the kids who decided one night to throw heavy things off a Thruway overpass, trying to see if they could hit passing cars, and ended up killing a woman driving down the highway.

But this murder struck an emotional chord outside of Ulster the others couldn't touch. Partly, it was because of the age of the kids involved: thirteen and fifteen. The country seemed in the midst of an epidemic of teenage violence. While teens were still a small percentage of those arrested for murder, various statistics emphasized the tremendous increase in young killers since the 1980s—a thirty percent boost in some studies. From 1986 to 1994, federal statistics showed an increase in violent crime arrests of 317.4 per hundred thousand to 527.4; murder arrests went from 6.4 to 14.5 per hundred thousand. As bad as the actual statistics were, a 1994 Gallup Poll found that most people thought the situation was far worse—with the majority of those polled believing that youths commit forty-three percent of all violent crimes in the U.S. The actual number at the time was around thirteen percent.

It was one thing for a murder to occur during a drug war in a blighted ghetto; it was quite another for the victim to be a grandmother in a quiet, middle-class town. Reduced to its essence—girl and boyfriend kill own grandma—the story elicited a universal one word reaction: *Why?*

The story gained national attention for a short while; even *The New York Times* ran stories. Television and radio were also interested. But after the initial shock and the trend stories about how terrible the young generation had become, interest began to wane. Saugerties was too small a place to stay in the spotlight very long. The outside media continued to cover the story, but only in outline form. For the most part, their editors felt they had already answered the "why" question—kids were rotten.

It fell to the local papers, the *Freeman* and the *Times Herald Record,* to stay with the case and do the real reporting.

In the days following the discovery of the murder, the papers' staffers fanned out to talk to neighbors and family members, the *de rigeur* modern response to violent death. When interviewed, most of the neighbors reacted with shock toward the murder, noting how "nice"—the word came up again and again—Betty Gardner was. They also called James Evans a bully, and seemed to feel that Wendy Gardner had gone sour under his influence. The neighborhood and thus their stories, put nearly all the blame on Evans .

But the day after the initial stories appeared, both the *Freeman* and the *Times Herald Record* printed stories that created an undercurrent of doubt that would bubble up through the trial. For the reporters had found James Evans' mother. And Dinah decided to tell them what Wendy had said about being abused by her grandmother. She also shared a few of the letters she had found from Wendy to James.

As quoted and paraphrased in the newspapers, the letters showed a girl whose life was troubled, one doing poorly in school and obsessed with sex. But none specifically backed up the accusations of abuse, and none of the information the reporters developed went beyond the "he said, she said" stage. Dinah Evans' statements also clearly implied that the teenagers—or at least Wendy—were or could be guilty of murder.

Still, bolstered by some initially ambiguous statements by Buzz Gardner that his mother was a "disciplinarian" whose actions might be seen as abuse, the papers decided to run the charges anyway. Jeff Storey, the managing editor of the *Times Herald Record,* felt that, since the teenagers were not there to speak for themselves—they were both being held on Long Island, out of press access—the parents were acceptable surrogates. At the time, the newspaper did not know that Dinah Evans and Buzz Gardner had had scrapes with the law; even if it had, the decision would probably have been the same.

At the *Kingston Freeman,* the editors and reporters were making pretty much the same decision, determined to get out as much of the story as possible. Though the *Times Herald Record* was a larger newspaper overall, with a circulation running to about a hundred thousand on Sundays, it was headquartered in the next county. The *Freeman* had a bigger circulation in Ulster County, and considered itself the paper of record there. As such, it specialized in day-to-day coverage, providing readers with nuts and bolts stories. And it was its "murder and mayhem" reporter—more officially known as cops and courts—Cynthia Werthamer who got the first interview with Buzz Gardner. It proved to be the only "in-depth" interview he gave to anyone during the entire ordeal.

Werthamer, a pixie-ish thirty-something journalist with a tour at AP under her belt, cut a jaunty figure in town, traveling the quarter-mile from her office to court on a bike. Athletic, with a personality that mixed a bit of beat reporter-tough guy with girlish sympathy, Werthamer would end up dogging the case for more than two years.

She located Buzz Gardner and showed up at his home near the village of New Paltz, then managed somehow to gain the volatile father's sympathy long enough for him to pour his heart out to her.

"I'm dying inside," he confessed. "I've lost everything I ever had."

The forty-four-year-old choked back tears as he blamed the death on his mother's physical and mental abuse of Wendy, and on Child Protective Services for failing to follow up complaints of abuse. He also claimed that he had tried to get custody of Wendy two weeks before the murder, but was turned down when he refused to agree to a blood test.

The story that evolved from the interview was a powerful one, but as the case progressed it would become obvious that it left out some important details. Gardner spoke of having agreed two years before to let his mother take custody. Court documents show that custody had been awarded about a decade before. Wendy's school record became "straight A's" rather than its actual B to B+ average before junior high. And the story skipped lightly over Buzz's own history and conflict with his mother, conceding only that he had not been an ideal parent. The story did not directly indicate that the test he had refused to take during the custody battle was for drugs.

Werthamer worked hard to verify what she could of the story. Handicapped by confidentiality laws, she could not see any of the family court records. A spokesman for Child Protective Services confirmed that there had been some family court activity, but noted smugly that all allegations are investigated, and that children are always removed from someone's custody when abuse is found. It was as if the agency was completely incapable of making a mistake.

Other family members contradicted Buzz Gardner's accusations of the grandmother's abuse, and hinted of his substance abuse problems. Werthamer included that information in the story, though what most people—the family especially—tended to remember were the accusations, not the contradictions.

Over at the *Times Herald Record,* the story was assigned to John Milgrim, a blond-haired, blue-eyed former architectural student who had discovered an aptitude for reporting a few years before during a failed run for public office. He'd been nicknamed "Migraine", partly a play on his name and partly a tribute to his persistence, by fellow staff members as well as some of the police and prosecutors who dealt with him on a regular basis. He had a fairly wide acquaintance not only with officials in Kingston but with policemen throughout the area. Early in his career, a story he had done had helped troopers link together a string of seemingly unrelated murders as the work of a single suspect. At times cocky and apt to beat his own drum, he could also seem disarmingly open, and even at times shy. Like nearly every other reporter who ever worked a beat, he kept irregular hours, working in long, unpredictable stretches when he thought he had a good story by the tail.

And the murder of Betty Gardner looked like just such a story.

The *Freeman*'s early reporting, with its interview from Buzz Gardner, was more detailed than the *Times Herald Record*'s, and it hinted at the complicated family situations. From their own reporting, Milgrim and his editors knew there was a lot more there. That, and the overwhelming question of "Why?" that was on everyone in the community's lips, led them to make an unusual decision: Milgrim would spend the next several weeks finding out everything he could about the murder. While still burdened with a few other assignments, his main job was to research the case.

The commitment of resources was unusual for a paper of the *Record*'s size. Its circulation is spread out among several counties and three states, and the Kingston office, charged with covering all of northern Ulster, consisted of exactly two reporters. Nonetheless, managing editor Storey thought the resources well-spent. Everyone, he said, wanted the "Why?" question answered.

* * *

Both the *Freeman* and the *Times Herald Record* asked psychiatrists, counselors, and therapists who were experts on youthful behavior to answer that question. Without most of the facts of the case—not even the prosecutors or defense lawyers had them yet—the therapists made a few general observations but were naturally unable to provide any real insight. They knew little of the specifics about the murder or the two children. This made for stories that said the experts were baffled by the teen lovers' behavior, adding to a general aura of shock over the murder but little in the way of insight about why it had occurred, the ostensible reason for the articles.

Storey admitted later he was dubious about doing those types of stories, realizing that they often led to little real insight. Nonetheless, it was something all newspapers did and their competitors at the *Freeman* had already gotten one in. The piece ran prominently in the *Record*.

None of the stories the newspapers or anyone else did on the murder carefully looked at the family court system, at the time largely enshrouded in mystery because of the laws allegedly protecting privacy. None of the stories, either immediately after the murder was discovered or over the long course of the trials, looked at the school district, which under state law had an important role to play in not only educating students but seeing that they got the support necessary to get that education. At no time were school officials called to task for having so obviously lost track of a young girl in trouble. None of the newspaper articles or television stories went into in-depth analysis on parenting or drug abuse. And it was left to a specialty publication, *American Lawyer,* two and a half years after the murder, to raise questions about the treatment of youths in the adult legal system.

What the stories did do was carry quite clearly the implication that the two youths, whose indictments were still fresh from the word processor, were guilty. While a story might use the words "charged," the way it was written made clear that the author and editors had already concluded the two teenagers were guilty. With their information largely based on what the police and district attorney told them—which not only came second-hand but apparently did not include the full confessions or most of the evidence—the media had disposed of the "presumed innocent" label in all but the most theoretical terms. The question reporters were trying to answer wasn't, "Why did Betty Gardner die?" but "Why did *these* teenagers commit the murder?"

20

Sucker-punched

Early January 1995

The top floor of the old Ulster County Court building was a domain unto itself, prowled by a man who, in fact as well as symbol, was at the top of the Ulster County justice scene. Even if he had been the kind of person who boasted aloud of his accomplishments, Mike Kavanaugh didn't have to. For he'd long since acquired the power—through reputation, longevity, and most of all ability—to shape more than mere perception. He was in many ways the very embodiment of justice in Ulster County.

Kavanaugh loved the power and responsibility. His zeal was one of the reasons the former Eagle Scout was so successful. For unlike a lot of other district attorneys around the state, Kavanaugh not only supervised cases but prosecuted the major ones himself. It made for a hell of a lot of work, and it made for a hell of a lot of success. The bottom line on Mike Kavanaugh was that he was a damn good prosecutor.

The public had first found out just how good more than two decades before, when some New York City mafia types had the audacity to kill and dump a surplus associate in the Ulster County woods. Then a young assistant, Kavanagh bit into the case harder than a Doberman nailing a trespasser. Men with shotguns guarded the entire city during the trial. When it was over, Tony "Pro" Provenzo, a mob prince until he met Kavanagh in court, was sent so far upstate his relatives needed a passport to visit.

None of the battles that followed seemed quite as daunting for the jaunty attorney, not even when he took on popular Democratic Governor Mario Cuomo in the 1980s after the governor made the mistake of granting amnesty to Gary McGivern, a man the DA had put away for killing a cop. Kavanagh, a Republican, couldn't do much about the governor, but he did have the last word on McGivern: he hounded him for months, then nailed his carcass to the wall when he violated parole.

Past cases didn't matter this morning in early January 1995. The DA was now concerned with a local murder and local justice. Kavanagh intended on presenting the Gardner murder to the grand jury himself, and as was his habit, he enlisted his most trusted aide, Don Williams, to head over to the crime scene with him and get a feel for what had happened.

Williams was a detail-oriented man probably as tough as his boss, though more of a background player because of circumstances. He handled a lot of murder cases himself. He often found himself serving as sounding board not just for Kavanagh but his subordinates. He was the kind of guy who could be trusted to tell you what he thought, not what he thought you wanted to hear.

Kavanagh, nearing fifty, loved being able to do things like this, going in and seeing what really happened close up.

Saugerties lay about twenty minutes north of Kingston, an easy straight drive up Route 9W. Kavanagh and Williams took the turn off the state highway near the diner where James Evans and Wendy Gardner had found the food too bloody to eat after the murder. The road behind the Great American plaza was still scarred with the "burn-outs" from the teenagers' night of showing off for friends, though the two prosecutors were too busy hunting for the address to notice.

The house, modest, simple, didn't announce itself as anything special. Yellow police tape marked it off, and state troopers were on hand to continue their search for any evidence missed in the first rush. The DA and the assistant got out of the car, walked up the white steps to the beige door, and went inside. Kavanagh tried to take everything in. He went up the short flight of steps to the living room, where he was immediately struck by the small Christmas tree. It seemed modest to him, not bare, but obviously the sort of tree erected by someone just getting by, struggling to give a piece of Christmas to two kids while on a limited budget. Murder was a terrible thing to happen to her. Anger began rising inside the prosecutor, a righteous anger that steeled him to seek justice for the victim. Talking about it to others might make it sound corny and old-fashioned—weepy-eyed emotion from a guy who all evidence suggested was tougher than a leatherneck hitting

Iwo Jima—but it was the sort of thing that kept the DA going.

Kavanagh shook his head, and he and Williams continued through the house, taking their survey. They glanced through the kitchen, walked down the hallway, saw the grandmother's room. Then he passed into Wendy Gardner's room.

Her teddy bear undid him. A simple, large, cuddly bear sat on the bed. A stuffed animal icon of childhood, Wendy's constant, sometimes only, companion, lay waiting for her to return.

Slowly, the dark Irish eyes worked around the rest of the room. It didn't—couldn't—wouldn't—belong to a homicidal monster. It was the room of a little girl, a lot like the rooms his daughters had lived in when they were growing up.

A little girl he no longer wanted to prosecute for murder, even as he realized it would be his duty to do so. The man who stood down the mob and hounded a governor got sucker-punched by a kid who didn't even know who he was.

Mike Kavanagh and Don Williams continued looking through the house. Among the things they found was the diary that Wendy had kept that summer, a diary that would prove critical to the case against her. But even though the DA would go ahead and make sure the grand jury returned a swift indictment, even as he worked overtime to bring the killers to justice, Kavanagh had second and third thoughts. Not about Evans—he was convinced from his background that the kid deserved to go behind bars for a very long time, maybe even longer than the law allowed. But Wendy seemed another matter.

Not because of the evidence, but because she was a girl.

Truly. It was sexist, it was hopelessly soft-hearted, it was maybe, in light of the facts that investigators would develop, absurd. But that was how Kavanaugh felt. He didn't want to prosecute a little girl for murder. As the case proceeded, he found an excuse to hand it off. The excuse was a valid one: a murder conviction in another case had been overturned and sent back for retrial because of a judge's error, but Kavanaugh clearly welcomed it. And as the case against the teenagers proceeded, he sent out occasional trial balloons about dealing with some leniency toward Wendy Gardner, either through a reduced charge or a plea bargain or asking for a lighter sentence if there was a conviction.

Most of the reaction in the community, where regular people could still accost the DA in a local store or on the street, was negative.

Under other circumstances, the trial of the two teenagers might have fallen to Don Williams, but he was busy with what would prove a sensational murder case involving a man in the city of Kingston. Instead, Kavanaugh turned to an assistant who had never tried a murder case for the office before, Mike Miranda. In his late forties with two girls around the age of the Gardner sisters, Miranda was a short, chain-smoking refugee from New York City who years before had fled upstate to become a country lawyer.

There was a lot of city left in his voice, the rhythm of an Italian-American neighborhood lingering in his

o's and a's. Hanging a shingle out in the old-boy world
of Ulster County law didn't feed the family too well; by
the mid 1980s Miranda was handling cases for the DA's
office on a part-time basis. When a full-time slot opened
up in 1988 he grabbed it.

Miranda ducked into his tiny office one day as a felony
drug case wound down. He was surprised to find a thick
manila folder on his desk. The folder contained material
on Betty Gardner's murder, his boss's way of "asking"
if he wanted the case. The grand jury had already voted
to indict. Miranda found the file and the case it represented meticulously prepared; he would later praise the
state police for doing a textbook job setting up the case.

But as he began to read the file, he realized the trial
wasn't going to be a cakewalk. James Evans looked pretty
solid, but Wendy Gardner came off very sweet and very
innocent, and she had been barely thirteen when the
murder went down. Miranda worried immediately about
jury nullification—a fancy way of saying that the jury
might feel so sorry for the kid that they'd let her walk,
or at least reduce the charge to something that
amounted to a slap on the wrist.

He didn't want to let that happen. Part of it was ego—
he had no intention of losing what amounted to his
biggest case here. But another part, a larger part, was
justice. For unlike his boss, Miranda didn't buy the little
girl stuff. His view had Wendy Gardner every bit as guilty
as James Evans.

He had to admit she looked angelic, and not just in
the photos that had appeared in the newspapers. But
the more Miranda looked at her diary, the more he
talked to her sister, the more he studied the statements
Gardner and Evans had given the police, the more he
was convinced the angel thing was bogus. Pressed, he

would admit she was one of the rare criminals who might be salvageable, but only after she did her time.

Miranda felt he had to win the case, and not just because it would mean a lot in the office or to his career. Frankly, even a stellar performance wasn't going to add up to much career-wise—he was way back in line to succeed Kavanagh. But this was the kind of case that bothered everybody. Killing your grandmother—it shook people as far away as Texas and California who read about it over breakfast or caught it on the nightly news before turning in. It shook people's faith in humanity, questioned their sense of justice. It was the kind of case you *had* to win.

There were a number of issues to be decided before the cases came to trial. Among the them was what to do with Andy Bender, the friend who had ridden with the killers after the murder and who had seen the body in the trunk. His help looking for a place to dump the body and the failure to notify the police that a murder had taken place could conceivably have amounted to a crime in itself. On the other hand, he could just as conceivably be an important witness in the case, since he had seen the body. And in the eyes of the law he was only a child himself.

The state troopers were not entirely sure where Bender fit in at first. For a brief moment it had seemed like he might have been involved in the actual killing, however they had ultimately held off filing any charges against him. There was some thought that he might be usable as a witness, though he came off as a wise guy and would later prove to have his own difficulties with the authorities.

Miranda had Andy Bender brought in to see what he knew. The assistant district attorney nearly fell out of his vinyl and chrome office chair when Bender confessed to having killed Betty Gardner himself.

With a gun.

Thing was, the kid seemed to believe it.

Any possibility of using Andy Bender as a witness pretty much vaporized there.

On Thursday, January 5, less than a week after Kathy Gardner had run from the house where she'd been kept prisoner, a grand jury voted to indict both James Evans and Wendy Gardner for the murder of Betty Gardner. The vote moved the case against the two teenagers from the town court, where preliminary hearings could have been held, to the more august chambers in the county courthouse at the center of Kingston. The grand jury's indictment meant only that there was enough evidence for the two to stand trial. It was the first step in the long process of determining their guilt or innocence.

More significant than the indictment itself was the fact that the teenagers were to stand trial as adults, not as children. Because of their ages, the district attorney could have chosen to bring their cases to family court, where different standards and penalties would have been invoked. While it is impossible to predict what might have happened there, the district attorney and most, if not all, of his staff believed that both Gardner and Evans would have gotten away with a light sentence if convicted in family court.

Though allowing them to be tried as adults, New York State law did draw one significant difference between the pair and adult defendants. Because they were under sixteen (James by only two weeks), the maximum sentence they could receive if found guilty was nine years to life in prison. Ordinarily, the sentence would have been twenty-five to life. At the time of the murder, New York did not have a death penalty.

Despite the quick indictment, there would be more than two years of delay and maneuvering before the pair were brought to trial. In the intervening months, Ulster would be hit with what was for the small county a spate of murders. Its lone county court judge had to preside not only over the murder cases, but other felonies as well. Those cases were part of the circumstances that led to the delays, somewhat unusual in the relatively small county.

James Evans and Wendy Gardner remained all that time in the custody of the state, locked in DFY facilities. Though Gardner's lawyer argued for "bail a thirteen-year-old could afford," the arguments for release never seemed very realistic. Neither teenager was ever granted bail.

21

Christian burial

January 5, 1995

The small organ shook the thick walls and narrow oak floorboards of Saint Mary of the Snow as the group of family, friends, and neighbors filtered into the church. The notes underlined the words of the entrance procession, "Jesus, remember me when you come into your Kingdom ..." The white walls were thick with shadows, and the candles flickered fitfully.

For Catholics, death can be interpreted as a joyous occasion. Believers hold that those who die have found eternal life in a better place. The rites and readings of the funeral mass are thick with references to eternal salvation and true peace. But it is difficult to put grief aside, and those here this morning could not do so easily. Injustice hung thick in the air. If one or two relatives were aware of Betty Gardner's own faults and sins, still they believed they could never have weighed against the awesome obscenities that had been done to her. Disbelief overwhelmed them, and memories, not just of Betty but of her granddaughter, played against the blank whiteness around the simple altar at the front. No one in the family wanted to believe Wendy had done this. More than a few of the celebrants at the mass, rising as the priest entered to sprinkle holy water, wondered if perhaps some minor thing they might have done would have changed this terrible history.

At the very back of the church, in the section nearest to the room reserved for confessions, sat Buzz Gardner. Segregated in fact as well as spirit from the rest of his family, he had nonetheless followed the twisted course of his relationship with his parents up this hillside to the solid space of these thick walls. Whatever else had happened between them, there were photos in the family album showing him and his mother smiling and happy. Whatever he might have said in the past to her, or say now to the press, about the abuse he thought had led to the murder, there were yet strands of duty and love, blood ties that could not be broken.

The church was small, and it was not difficult to see his daughter Kathy at the front, flanked by other family members, including the great-aunt and uncle she had gone to live with. Buzz's decision to stay at Wendy's side had effectively cut him away from hers. His decision to accuse his mother of abuse and to speak his mind about her had severed whatever ties remained between him and the rest of the family. No one had spoken to him at the wake, no one would speak to him now, and he did not push the issue.

The accusations of abuse had been denied in a terse prepared statement released to the press after Buzz

Gardner's interview. The statement represented the family's interpretation of what had happened, putting most, if not all, of the blame on James Evans.

"Betty Gardner's life was taken because she tried to protect her granddaughter from the damaging influence of James Evans," they wrote. "She raised her granddaughters for nine years. Any accusations by James Evans, his family, Wendy Gardner or Clarence Gardner are absolutely untrue. Accusations of abuse were fabricated only after [Betty] tried unsuccessfully to stop Wendy from seeing James, and are currently being used in an attempt to rationalize the heinous criminal act which ended Betty Gardner's life."

It was the only public comment family members would make before the trial, and practically the only comment they would ever make. Despite the intense media interest, the family decided not to grant any interviews.

Most though not all of the neighbors expressed extreme skepticism about the charges of abuse; a few others said it was mainly a matter of interpretation.

One family member absent from the funeral would not have been welcome under any circumstance, not even if she stayed in the back row.

Twenty miles south in a dilapidated old house in the worst section of the City of Poughkeepsie, Wendy's mother Jann sat in front of a broken television set, staring at the photo of her two girls atop it. Her body had been ravaged by years of self-abuse. Her mind was worn away, slipping and sliding through unreal shadows of consciousness. A lot of days she didn't bother eating.

Months before, she had gotten a letter from Wendy.

She'd read it, ripped it up, then tossed the pieces into the back lot with the rest of the trash.

I hate you, Wendy had written, *but I think about you. You ruined my life, bitch.*

Jann pulled the battered blazer she'd gotten from the Salvation Army thrift shop a few blocks away a bit tighter against the January cold.

Wendy's grandmother loomed out of the blackness of the detention center cell. Before James Evans could ask how she got there, before he could say anything, she was screaming at him, calling him useless and worse, and kicking him. He tried to protect himself but she was too powerful, incredibly strong. He fell from the bed as she lunged at him and he felt her kicking at him. James tried to fend her off but was helpless, impotent as a baby, pounded by feet and hands and arms and fists, pounded to a pulp. Wendy was laughing in the background. Kathy was laughing in the background. Everyone was laughing as he rolled on the floor, blood pouring from his wounds.

It took forever to realize it was a dream.

As the final echo of music filtered from the open doors of the church, Betty Gardner's body was placed into the hearse. Family members slipped into a gray limousine, and a procession of cars wound down through the village, passing the ruins of Henry Barclay's faded utopia, down toward the flat land where the St. Mary's cemetery was located. The stone rows that spread out around the flagpole were crowded with the modest markers of working men and women. Like those in cemeteries around the world, they told their stories with simple pathos, a few chiseled words and dates summing up lifetimes.

The procession moved slowly to the north side of the stone garden, proceeding inevitably toward the pile of dirt that marked the fresh grave. The home where Betty Gardner had lived and died lay within an easy walk. The week before, her body had circled this ground several times, hulked in the trunk of her old Mercury, hugging a spare tire.

The stone that marked her grave might count as one of the more elaborate in the St. Mary of the Snow Cemetery, though in truth it was rather simple. Jesus knelt next to the family name. He was risen from the sepulcher, reminding the faithful that they, too, would have their moment of peace. Beneath Christ, "1927 Elizabeth 1994" would be chiseled. There would be no mention of the trials she had endured, no note of accomplishments, loves, desires, fears, and above all, no allusion to the way she died. These no longer mattered to Elizabeth "Betty" Murphy Gardner. When the soul departs, the body returns to dust and nothing else ever really matters, except to those left behind.

When the last mourner left the cemetery, the workers got busy. Gently, Betty Gardner was placed in the ground next to her husband, the man she'd missed so strongly all these years. They had been apart an interminable time, some of it good, some of it bad, much of it difficult.

As a Catholic, Betty believed that her soul separated from her body at the moment of death, and that by now her true essence had risen to be judged and assigned its eternal fate. It was her body's turn now; after the obscenity of the past week, it had finally found peace.

22

"I don't know why . . ."

January 1995

Shortly before noon on January 12, Ulster County Court Judge J. Michael Bruhn listened impassively at the bench as James Evans' lawyer Dan Gaffney pleaded to let his client stay at the Nassau County Youth Detention Center. Evans was receiving counseling there, Gaffney argued; he should stay there and get the help he needed. The lawyer stood in much the same spot with much the same posture he had used a short time before as he entered a plea of not guilty to the murder charge.

Celebrating his sixteenth birthday that day, Evans was now old enough by state law to be sent to the Ulster County Jail. There were a myriad of reasons for transferring him there, not least of which was to save the county considerable expense.

"One of the realities of the criminal justice system

is, you don't get to pick your spot," declared Bruhn, denying the lawyer's request.

Privately, James Evans had little use for the counseling, or at least would admit to none. He wanted to stay at Nassau because that was where Wendy was. As the judge announced his decision, the two young lovers turned toward each other in the courtroom. Wendy Gardner, a large crucifix dangling in front of her pullover prison shirt, nearly began to cry. James reached out and for a brief moment the two lovers held hands. It was the last time they would ever do so.

The sheriff's deputies began escorting them away. Dinah Evans went toward the deputies, holding out an envelope.

"It's his birthday," she tried to explain.

The deputies wouldn't let her give him the card, but she leaned in and kissed him good-bye. She gave a small picture to another deputy, asking him to convey it to her son.

It was a snapshot of Wendy and James together.

Whatever effect the counseling may or may not have had, the transfer to Ulster County Jail hurt James Evans in a way he could never have expected, for it made him much more accessible to the press. When John Milgrim of the *Times Herald Record* showed up to interview him, the sixteen-year-old agreed to talk to the reporter.

Milgrim had already done a considerable amount of research for his story on why James and Wendy had committed the murder. Among his sources was Dinah Evans, who had told him of some of the family court battles. He had also talked to kids in the neighborhood, had gone to James' father's hometown, and had seen at least part of the teenager's family court records, ostensibly closed to the public. He viewed Evans as a bully. The boy reminded him of a childhood acquaintance, since jailed for a felony, who liked to hurt other kids for the pleasure of seeing them in pain.

Obtaining the interview was a serious coup; anything James Evans said would be big news.

Barely five-six, Milgrim liked to play the role of tough guy reporter, but at first found the teenager unresponsive to his badgering style. So the twenty-eight-year-old journalist began a kind of boasting talk of his own alleged juvenile delinquency, in effect daring James to match his exploits. James gradually began answering questions.

As printed in the newspaper after the interview, the story James Evans told paralleled what he had said to the state police about the murder. He had been popping amphetamines and drinking vodka and orange juice out of a gallon jug, *á la* the rap music he'd been listening to. Wendy and her grandmother had been arguing, and something inside him snapped.

Milgrim heard Evans not only confess to the crime but predict that he would get at least ten years in jail (the maximum sentence possible was actually nine years to life), facts which would play prominently in the story he wrote.

The reporter asked Evans about some of the incidents in the neighborhood the kids had told him about, stories that made him look like a bully. When he came to one about microwaving two of his mother's cats, Evans reacted with surprise, denying it.

Then he recovered his boasting posture. "People do call me the king of the microwave."

Milgrim thought he saw him wink and included the

incident, with the denial though not the wink, in a later story. The anecdote about killing cats, told by different people in different versions, always secondhand, and actually a classic suburban legend collected by contemporary anthropologists, came to symbolize much of Evans' personality as presented to the public. Cruelty to animals as a youth is an alleged hallmark of serial killers; someone who does it and winks about it surely is evil incarnate.

James Evans later told his mother that he had been severely misquoted throughout the story, that Milgrim had asked him a series of questions which he refused to answer, and to finally get him off his back he said, "I don't know why any of it happened." That response, he claimed, somehow got twisted into a confession of murder.

Dan Gaffney was angered when the interview with James Evans appeared in the paper. It had been done against his advice, without his consent, and it mocked the not-guilty plea he had entered on behalf of his client just a few days earlier. Worse, it made it more difficult to defend him.

By this time, Gaffney did not harbor any doubts about how hard that would be. Evans had, after all, essentially admitted he had killed Betty Gardner when the state police interrogated him. But Gaffney had to fashion some sort of defense for the teenager, and newspaper stories proclaiming his guilt weren't exactly helpful.

If the confession was bad, Milgrim's "why they did it" story, which appeared the following Sunday, was worse. Spread over three pages and bylined with Mark Pittman, one of Milgrim's editors, the story was heavily influenced by Evans' "confession" to Milgrim and played the youths' love affair prominently. It touched on James' family court history and played up neighbors' accusations of Evans as the neighborhood bully. The poverty of Evans' early days was included, but rather than mitigating the defendant's circumstances, it reinforced the impression of a life gone horribly wrong.

Most readers would probably conclude from the story that James Evans was an out-of-control kid who had been soured by a hard early life and poor upbringing, a time bomb who twisted Wendy Gardner toward evil, then killed Betty Gardner in a drunken haze, partly out of anger and partly because he wanted to have sex with her granddaughter twenty-four hours a day. A few might wonder why his relationship with Wendy had been so special that it led to murder. But the unmistakable impression any reader would draw from the story was that James Evans was guilty of the crime beyond any doubt, reasonable or otherwise.

Wendy Gardner got off much easier. Perhaps one reason was that she was not made available for an interview, nor was detailed information about her easy to gather. Jerry Flaherty was already working hard to stage-manage her public image. Her family court involvement, comparatively minor, remained closed and inaccessible, and local school district officials were not talking. The only relative of Gardner's willing to speak about her was her mother, a drug addict who hadn't seen her in years. In any event, the story fell into line with the general direction the Gardner family statement had taken: the bully of Barclay Heights was largely responsible for the murder. Wendy's early days with Buzz and Jann (misspelled as Jan) were noted, and she was again called a "straight A student." The accusations of abuse were also included, as were neighbors' various opinions about them, but Betty Gardner was primarily presented as "the only stable influence" in her life, and thus an obstacle to Evans' influence and pleasure.

The publicity was bad enough, but now Gaffney had to worry that the prosecution would call Milgrim to the stand during the trial and ask about the confession. There would be almost no way to counter such a tactic.

But the story was hardly the only frustrating development in the case for Dan Gaffney. After hearing of the accusations of abuse by Betty Gardner, he obtained subpoenas demanding that the Department of Social Services turn over all of its paperwork on the charges.

No documents were ever found. Despite the fact that there were elliptical references to charges and investigations in the reports by counselors dealing with James Evans, the claims of physical abuse later presented in court amounted mostly to isolated incidents and second-hand accounts. The lawyer soon concluded that the questions of abuse were a can of worms that could as easily work against James as for him.

Self-defense or any sort of justifiable homicide defense wasn't going to work. In Gaffney's opinion, his client had only one real hope, an obscure, even vague escape hatch in New York law that lets a jury opt for a lesser charge if a murder is perpetrated by someone who is extremely emotionally disturbed. In the parlance of the law, the defense is called "extreme emotional disturbance."

Extreme emotional disturbance is considered an affirmative defense since the person using it must prove to the jury that the condition exists, unlike the standard courtroom defense, where the burden of proof is on the prosecution. It does not result in a not guilty verdict either. Instead, it reduces second degree murder (premeditated killing) to manslaughter, which carries a lighter prison sentence. In layman's terms, it allows a defendant to say, *Yes, I did plan to kill this person, but there were mitigating circumstances that made me think I was justified.*

For a jury to find extreme emotional disturbance, jurors must be convinced that extreme emotions caused the defendant to kill. They must also find that there was a reasonable explanation for those emotions. In cases where this defense has been successfully used, a history of abuse, for example, has been persuasive. The jurors must also find that because of the extreme emotions the defendant felt, in his or her opinion, that murder was a reasonable act.

Defining the defense can be difficult, even for lawyers, since it is so open to interpretation. It has meant different things to different juries. It might, for example, be used in a case where an abused child could cite years of abuse as contributing to an emotional disturbance.

Gaffney reasoned it might fit this case. James Evans had had a difficult early life. Perhaps something there had led him to think murder was justifiable.

There had also been all those claims from Wendy Gardner that she was being abused. It was clear from the attorney's interviews with him that James thought he was protecting her.

Maybe that was the key.

It was a tricky, almost desperate ploy, since it called for the defense to admit guilt, then try to excuse it. It would almost certainly rely on the testimony of at least one expert psychological witness. And that witness had to be extremely persuasive.

Dan Gaffney began searching around for such an expert. He got the name of Theodore Sabot from an Albany attorney he admired, and contacted him.

If the early publicity had hurt James Evans in the court of public opinion, it had played somewhat more favorably for Wendy Gardner. She did, after all, have certain natural advantages: she was a girl, she was younger, and in sharp contrast to James, the face she showed the world was quiet, demure, and innocent.

She also had a hell of an attorney.

Jerry Flaherty had begun waging war for Gardner from the moment of her preliminary hearing, loudly proclaiming her innocence in the best traditions of the criminal bar. Flaherty didn't just ask for bail, he suggested that she be granted bail "appropriate for a thirteen-year-old" or placed under house arrest with an electronic bracelet, an action generally reserved for those accused of very minor offenses. He compared her confinement on Long Island to being sent to Siberia.

It was not that Flaherty expected to win most, or maybe any, of these battles, though he never, ever, admitted that on the record to anybody. His actions were part of a concerted effort to remind the general public, and any potential jurors—maybe even the prosecution and judge—that his client was a young girl. He had a family friend bring a teddy bear to the town court, where he was sure that photographers would snap a picture of her with it. (He later demurred from taking full credit for the ploy, which some thought was a bit too cute.) If the DA said the murder was premeditated,

Flaherty claimed just as loudly that his client had nothing to do with the crime.

While the lawyer was just doing what came naturally, he was motivated at least partly by a genuine concern for his client that went beyond mere professionalism. In his opinion, he had stumbled on a shell-shocked waif who had only a hazy notion of the great legal maw she was locked in. While his view became somewhat more complex as the case proceeded, the little girl he first met in a lonely room on a cold day in January before the arraignment haunted him long after the case went to trial.

With the ink on the arraignment barely dry, the experienced attorney had already settled on the outlines of his defense tactics. As much as possible, he would lay the blame on James Evans. Jurors needed to see a villain, and the teenage boy was perfectly suited for the role. One had only to look at John Milgrim's story. In fact, Milgrim's name would later appear on the list of witnesses Flaherty was considering calling, though that may have been more a diversionary tactic.

Pointing at another villain was only part of the defense, of course. Jeremiah Flaherty would have to counter the fact that Wendy had been in the house, had talked of the murder, had held and dragged her sister upstairs while Evans had killed Betty Gardner, and had then implicated herself in her long confession to the police. It was easy to present an image of innocence before the trial, since the most incriminating evidence was being held back by the prosecution. In front of a jury, things were going to be difficult.

For a tough guy from the West Side who would sooner get knifed in the gut than lose a murder case, it was a thorny problem to consider.

VI

EMOTIONAL DISTURBANCE

23

"All of the threads"

Fall 1995

After the rush of activity and publicity immediately following the discovery of Betty Gardner's body, the judicial system went into slow-motion. A routine motion separating the single case into two—one against James, one against Wendy—was granted. Psychological studies were requested for both defendants; neither defense counsel could proceed until they were completed. The small county court groaned under the workload of an unusual spate of criminal activity.

Finally, in September 1995, defense attorney Dan Gaffney received a report from Theodore J. Sabot, M.D., on James Evans. Though he already knew the broad outlines of the report and the material it was based on, the sixteen single-spaced pages filled Gaffney with real hope about the case—not that he might manage to get

James off, but that a bid for "emotional disturbance" and the conviction of manslaughter instead of murder might prevail.

Dr. Sabot had spent a total of eleven hours over three sessions interviewing Evans in Gaffney's office. While it might not sound like enough, it was nearly three times the length the prosecution's psychological expert spent with Evans, and in fact, it was an unusually long time, even in a murder case. Sabot had also studied a mountain of other reports and evaluations done on James over the years. He was without exaggeration an expert on James Evans and what had caused him to commit murder.

The psychiatrist's conclusion, however, was not surprising. He had been hired to find anything that might have mitigated Evans' guilt, and that's what he did. But his report stated the case more strongly than even Gaffney could have dreamed when he first contacted Sabot in late January. It was a persuasive and authoritative analysis of a teenage murderer.

"All of the threads of [James'] unhappy and violence-filled life had come together in a sudden and unplanned act," Sabot declared, "in which he blindly and reflexively, unintentionally killed to protect his beloved Wendy and to express all the pent-up rage of his awful life."

The psychiatrist laid out details of James' upbringing and family history, beginning with his mother's own childhood, which Sabot said included an alcoholic father and a violent mother. James' father, the report claimed, had been a heavy drinker; his mother had had a variety of legal problems, and had not been a constant presence in his life until he was about six years old. The custody battle was mentioned, and Sabot emphasized several incidents of violence not only by James' father but by his older brother that had occurred when James was growing up. In all of these cases, the psychiatrist said, the little boy watched in terror as a woman or girl was beaten. By age eleven, he not only knew this was wrong, but tried in his own way to stop it, including once throwing a plate at his brother, according to the psychiatrist.

"The theme of James being helpless in the face of violence towards women is an important and recurring one," wrote Sabot, "as well as his growing determination to prevent it when he was older."

A relationship with his paternal grandmother was cited to show that, whatever the prosecution's arguments, James Evans actually held most older people in high regard. The accounts of cruelty to animals were countered by evidence in the files from before the murder that James in fact did not want to hurt animals and was opposed to hunting. A previous report claiming that his bullying was a strategy to protect others was cited and reinforced.

Dr. Sabot did not paint the portrait of an angel. He mentioned Evans' behavior problems, and also his problems at the group home. The fifteen-year-old had been becoming increasingly depressed as well as hard to handle, the psychiatrist had pointed out. He also noted that James' behavior and disposition had gone downhill since early in 1994, "despite what seemed like an entire agency of therapists and caseworkers who might have had difficulty avoiding tripping over each other in their wish to help James. In addition to a caseworker, a family therapist, a probation officer, and family specialist were all working with the Evans family, and at least three agencies, DSS, CSS and SPAN were represented in these efforts. Nevertheless, on November 16, 1994, one professional . . . noted 'rapid deterioration' in the youngster's situation.''

But for Sabot, the "conduct disorder" that characterized much of Evans' interaction with the outside world "has been a protective facade for a chronic angry, bitter and despairing depression—a not uncommon phenomenon when so-called delinquents are given in-depth clinical assessments." James' interactions with family court and social service workers had been a succession of failed opportunities to deal with that depression—with devastating results.

As Sabot told it, the only good thing that had happened to James Evans from the boy's point of view in 1994 was his relationship with Wendy Gardner. According to the psychiatrist, when Wendy told James her grandmother was abusing her, he got "a weird churning feeling" in his stomach. While at first reluctant to believe that Betty Gardner had abused or was abusing Wendy—the report made clear that many of the incidents he was told about had allegedly occurred before they had started going together—James overheard Betty tell Wendy on the phone that she could smack her any time she wanted. After a while, he had to believe the stories.

"I couldn't handle this, couldn't handle anyone hurting Wendy," Evans had told Sabot during the interviews. The boy had been close to tears. "She was so perfect."

The psychiatrist was able to relate previous blackouts to the one described in James' statement to the police about the night of the murder, and said that the suspect still did not have a complete memory of what had happened. He reported that though James still loved Wendy, he was angry as well; he felt she had manipulated him into a situation where she knew he would lose control.

The report read like a psychological thriller, building to the murder and opening a window into James Evans' psyche. Its importance to Dan Gaffney was perhaps not so much in its findings but in the way it wove together James's extensive history to support them. The document, which would provide the basis for Gaffney's examination of Dr. Sabot on the witness stand, was an explicit and clear argument for manslaughter and its lesser penalty of three and a half to ten years, rather than murder and nine to life.

Finished reading the document, the attorney set it down on the glass top of his desk, obscuring a few of the dozens of snapshots of his family he kept there. Jurors needed a story, he realized, and Theodore Sabot had just given him a powerful one.

The defense strategy crystallized with the report. The prosecution would make its case, proving the murder. Then Gaffney would bring up his lone witness, a man who had spent a considerable time with the defendant, who was a real a psychiatrist with a long resumé and years of practice, a man who would weave a long and convincing description of James' sorry life and deluded self-image as savior.

The strategy meant that Gaffney couldn't dispute the bare facts of the murder too strenuously, but that was pretty much a foregone conclusion anyway, given the evidence. What he would do would be to work for James' interpretation of those facts. The kid lost his temper and went crazy—exactly what he told the police, what in fact he had told everyone. But from his extremely disturbed point of view, there was a reasonable explanation for the action.

The prosecution would undoubtedly present its own psychological expert on rebuttal to claim that this was just old-fashioned, cold-blooded murder, no special circumstances or fancy get-off-the-hook legal technicalities involved. But Gaffney could deal with that.

The district attorney's psychiatric witness was a good local fella, a nice guy, and competent by all means. He testified for the prosecution all the time. A sincere, local, small-town guy. Gaffney's witness had worked in California as well as New York, lectured at a state university, and was a bona fide national expert. The cream of the cream with no axe to grind, in Gaffney's eyes.

The desk's glass top caught the reflection of the lawyer's smile in the light, as he relished the prospect.

24

"Do you have Lexis?"

Spring 1996

Prosecutor Mike Miranda shifted restlessly against the low stone wall outside the county courthouse, smoking a cigarette. It was a pose and post he took often, as any of the guards who manned the metal detector at the nearby entrance could attest. There was no smoking allowed inside the building.

Besides, Miranda's energy wasn't the kind best confined to the small office he was assigned on the second floor. He was more a peripatetic ruminator, given to moving around and expending the adrenaline building up inside as he contemplated a case.

There was a lot to contemplate at the moment. Gaffney had rejected a plea bargain offer of seven years to life for Evans. That wasn't exactly the world's biggest surprise; the offer was a pittance, in practical terms affecting only the earliest date the kid could be considered for parole.

Correction, *rejected* for parole.

The real thing that bothered Miranda about the case was Dr. Sabot's report. "Bothered" didn't quite describe his feelings; the word didn't contain the proper degree of loathing.

It wasn't just that the assistant DA disagreed with the findings; he'd pretty much expected to, just as he figured Gaffney would find his own expert's report off-base. It went way beyond that.

Miranda, like a lot of members of the DA's office thought Sabot was little more than a hired gun making excuses for the defense.

It was a harsh opinion. Maybe that was a necessary part of psyching up for a case, though Miranda liked to think he didn't have to hate his opponent to do a good job in court. He had to admit, though, he really wanted a shot at James Evans on the stand. Oh, he would relish that—Evans on cross-examination, claiming to be a protector of little girls?

Miranda would tear him apart and the jury would see a sociopathic killer on the stand, a young man who could coldly wrap his over-sized paws around a grandmother's sweet neck and hold on until she was dead, dead, dead. There would be no mistaking that James Evans killed Betty Gardner when he got finished with the cross-examination. One or two of the jurors might even fear for his own life.

But Miranda knew that wasn't going to happen. Gaffney was too smart to let him near his client. The defense lawyer knew what the teenager would look like on the stand.

No, Miranda realized as he took a pull on the cigarette, no way he was going to have that much fun. And he did have a real problem. Sabot's report tied everything up in a tremendous bow for the jury.

Sure, he'd have his own psychiatric examination, but there was no guarantee that the jury was going to buy it.

The assistant DA had never dealt with Sabot before. And his damn report, at sixteen pages, was more detailed than any he'd ever seen.

Mike Miranda didn't use the word "persuasive," not even in his private thoughts.

He lit another cigarette before heading back to work through a side door.

Upstairs, Miranda pondered the report further. Most expert witnesses who testified in Ulster County Court were well-known to both the prosecution and the defense. For those who weren't, it was routine to call the DA's office in the expert's home county and see what they were like. The call was a courtesy. Sometimes it gave you a hint of how to handle the witness; more often it resulted in vague descriptions like "nice guy" or "favors the defense."

But never had it resulted in silence.

Miranda looked at the phone, then asked the Assistant Albany County District Attorney if he was still there.

"Hold on a minute," came the response. "Better yet, can I have your number?"

Puzzled, Miranda gave it to him and hung up.

A few minutes later, someone else in the Albany office called him back.

"Do you have Lexis-Nexis?" the caller asked.

"Sure," said Miranda, who knew there was a connection to the online computerized legal research service somewhere in the courthouse, but wasn't sure how it worked. "But—"

The caller gave him a reference number to a California case to type into the retrieval system, then hung up. Miranda went downstairs to a computer hooked up to Lexis and did what he was told.

Information burped up onto the screen.

"Holy shit," he shouted as he started to read. "Holy shit."

Theodore J. Sabot, star witness for the James Evans defense, was a convicted felon.

Sabot had pleaded guilty in California court in January 1985 to charges of grand theft and filing fraudulent state insurance claims. While the state had originally charged him with stealing $400,000 from its public insurance program, the plea admitted to approximately $100,000. The psychiatrist had served about two and a half years in prison, winning parole in September 1987. His license to practice medicine in New York, suspended in the wake of the conviction, wasn't renewed until November 1990.

As a summary of the California case began to spew from the printer, Mike Miranda ran back upstairs to find Don Williams. Though it did not contradict the lengthy report Sabot had prepared, or even address his competence as a doctor, the conviction would greatly undermine the psychiatrist's credibility. The fact that no mention of it was included in his curriculum vitae or resumé would give the prosecution, at the very least, an opening to embarrass him and upend the defense's strongest weapon.

"This is not your doctor," said Williams as he looked at the report.

"Shit, yeah."

They huddled for some time, discussing the conviction and its implications. It seemed clear to Miranda that Dan Gaffney didn't know about it; no defense attorney in his right mind would walk into a trap like this. Past convictions rarely if ever came up during discussions with a potential expert witness. Frankly, professionals like doctors, and lawyers for that matter, enjoyed an almost prejudicial assumption that they were above nasty things like felonies.

Had the information Miranda discovered been a critical piece of evidence—a murder weapon, for example—there was no question that the DA's office would be required to notify the defense of its existence, even if doing so would harm the prosecution's case. But in this instance, Miranda, Williams, and the other people they consulted felt that there was no such obligation. Miranda reasoned that it was not his responsibility to defend James Evans, nor had he chosen the expert in the first place. On the other hand, he realized that his boss, Mike Kavanagh, and Dan Gaffney were old friends. If Kavanagh caught wind of this, he might feel obligated out of friendship to tip Gaffney off. People might think of the DA as old blood and guts, but he didn't like to embarrass friends.

Williams and Miranda decided to keep the information from reaching Kavanagh. It was probably the one case in his long history that the DA knew less about than his assistants.

                        *   *   *

It turned out that the lawyers in the Albany County
District Attorney's Office had known about Dr. Sabot's
conviction for some time, but had held back on using
the information in any cases he was involved in. They
apparently wanted to save it for something important.

Mike Miranda, with three weeks left before opening
arguments were scheduled to begin, felt confident now
that he had the Sabot bombshell. Still, he put in a
mountain of overtime—unpaid, part of the job,
expected—preparing the case. For nearly two weeks,
he sifted through the files in the big boxes cluttering
a corner of his office, studying James Evans' history. He
wanted to be ready to counter any argument that might
be raised about Evans' emotional state, even before
launching the nuke.

During his breaks, Miranda couldn't help but think
about his daughters, now eleven and sixteen. Their pictures were up on the shelves where he kept a few legal
reference works, along with an old stereo that was rarely
if ever used. They were good girls, not perfect, of course,
but with a strong sense of right and wrong. They
believed in things.

But this was the kind of case that shook what you
believed in. That was why it was important to win, for
them, for him, for everyone.

25

"James Evans is responsible"

July 15-19, 1996

The Ulster County Courthouse stands in the center of the historic city of Kingston, not far from the site where New York's revolutionary congress debated and adopted the state constitution. The sometimes cantankerous group of rebels had fled north from New York City and Westchester in the face of the British advance in 1776. Among their less noted achievements at Kingston was the declaration that smoking be allowed in the convention chamber, ostensibly as a health measure.

In the early fall of 1777, a large British army under General Burgoyne began to falter in its drive south from Canada near present-day Saratoga. Somewhat belatedly, a rescue operation was mounted from New York City by Sir Henry Clinton, who sailed a large force up the Hudson River past rebel lines. By October, it was obvious to Clinton that his effort would fail, and so the British general decided to exact a bit of revenge by burning the revolutionaries' capital and houses nearby. It was a wanton act of destruction against civilians; Kingston had no military value, and only homes of the rebels were singled out in the initial wave of destruction. Accounts of exactly how much was lost in the great fire that resulted vary, but most contemporary sources put the destruction at near absolute.

The razing was merely the most graphic example of the area's long and violent early history. More than a hundred years before, Dutch settlers wrestled the countryside from the Mohawks and other natives in a bloody war that featured atrocities on both sides. If violence had become less monumental since the stones of the courthouse were first laid in the nineteenth century, the building itself could attest to the unending parade of passions and bloodletting that had continued unabated to modern times.

And so, though he was probably the youngest man ever charged with murder in Ulster County court, James Evans was just the latest in a long series of defendants brought before the bar accused of killing someone. If the details of his charges were particularly heartless, they fit within a context of acts perpetrated by supposedly civilized men for hundreds and thousands of years.

The trial judge was J. Michael Bruhn, a former Kingston city judge who had taken over the county court in 1994. He replaced Judge Francis Vogt, a local legend with enough of a sense of humor to leave his empty shoes for Bruhn under the bench. With more than twenty-five years of experience as a lawyer and a decade as a city judge, Bruhn was new but not a novice when the Evans trial began. His style in court tended to be laid-back but legally correct; when he instructed juries on knotty matters, he could include enough legal references to fill a law student's study guide. His style in sentencing, where like all judges he was severely restricted by state guidelines, seemed to vary from case to case.

During his first year on the county bench, he'd sentenced a nineteen-year-old to seventeen and half years to life in prison for killing an eighty-nine-year-old small town motel owner in a burglary. He told the teenager the sentence might not even be severe enough because "you are still alive." But the February before James Evans went on trial, Bruhn was severely criticized by anti-DWI groups for a supposedly light sentence—sixty days in jail, probation and community service—he gave to a teen who had killed his best friend in a DWI-related accident. Bruhn explained that he wanted to give the young man a chance to redeem himself. Afterwards, when the teenager violated his probation, the judge upped his sentence to two and a third to seven years in prison.

Despite the criticism, the judge told a local reporter that his feelings on the DWI sentencing hadn't changed. He felt his job was to do what the public wanted done— the whole public, not just one or another interest groups.

Around the time of the trial, there was some sentiment that Bruhn was still feeling his way on the bench. But most attorneys in town used words like "compassionate" and "fair" when describing him. Open in manner, the avid golfer and collector of antique clocks could be unassuming with visitors. With no objection from either the defense or prosecution, he decided the Evans and Gardner trials would be open to cameras, an option in the state at the judge's discretion. He felt strongly that the public should have access to the courts. Bruhn had dealt with many of the reporters who would cover the trial. He felt that they were unobtrusive and cooperative enough not to present any problems. It was one of the benefits of a small community; everyone knew each other and tried to get along. While the jury would not be sequestered, Bruhn decided the normal admonishments about avoiding news coverage and the like would suffice.

There was one external factor somewhat beyond the judge's control. The county had embarked on a plan to renovate the old courthouse, work that included ripping down walls and relocating a number of offices, as well as courtrooms. At times, the construction caused considerable inconvenience. Though the judge and contractors arranged a schedule to keep distractions to a minimum, a few people literally as well as figuratively tripped over power cords en route to the courtroom.

Jury selection in James Evans' murder case began July 15, shortly before noon. It proceeded quickly and by 4:30 P.M. the next afternoon, a dozen men and women had assured the judge they knew of nothing that would impair their ability to give Evans a fair hearing.

Opening arguments began at 10:35 A.M. July 17. Mike Miranda's hands chopped at the air as he described Betty Gardner's death as a "well-planned, brutal execution." The assistant district attorney confessed that he wasn't precisely sure why James Evans had killed the sixty-seven-year-old grandmother. Maybe, the assistant DA opined, it was revenge, maybe it was lust for her granddaughter. But he hammered home the savagery of the crime, telling the eight men and four women in the crowded jury box that James and Wendy had stuffed Betty Gardner's body in the trunk of her car and gone on to have some fun after killing her.

Miranda's opening statement was short, to the point, and lasted less than ten minutes. Through it all, James stared at the defense table, his head in his hands.

Dan Gaffney rose and began addressing the jury. His first words surprised them.

"I want to begin this case by stating there is no question whether or not James Evans committed a homicide," said Gaffney, firing the first blow in what he hoped was going to be a successful battle to win leniency for his teenage client. "James Evans is responsible for the death of Betty Gardner."

Silent before, the courtroom seemed to grow quieter as Gaffney let the point sink in. Every trial lawyer has a bit of actor in him. The trick is not to let it go too far. Gaffney waited just a second or two before adding the "but" that his whole case turned on.

James, he explained, had only killed because he was suffering emotional distress—the legal term was extreme emotional disturbance. Gaffney told the jurors to expect to hear from an accomplished psychiatrist who had spent considerable time examining James. The psychiatrist would explain what had led to the crime.

"He will testify to a horrendous, horrible home life," said Gaffney, ticking off some of the high points of Dr. Sabot's report. The lawyer tried to balance rhetoric against plain language; he tried to concentrate on giving the jurors a simple explanation they could use to justify a verdict of manslaughter. As Gaffney spoke, jurors glanced at his client sitting alone at the defense table, wearing a white shirt and tie. Now barely eighteen, he sat with his shoulders sunken beneath a gaunt face, looking hardly much of a villain at all.

In the audience, Dinah Evans steamed as Dan Gaffney worked through his long opening speech. For as he made his points about James' poor upbringing, he criticized her again and again, directly and indirectly.

As much as she wanted her son to go free, she felt what his lawyer was saying about her was exaggerated and worse. It was true that James had been the subject of a heated custody battle, but to her way of thinking, the fault for that lay with his father and the courts, not her. In her heart, she believed that she had done her best—and her other kids had done their best—to give James a stable life. And now Gaffney was telling the jurors that she hadn't, that she was, as the psychiatrist had said, a bad, even horrible mother.

Worse, the lawyer seemed to be staying away from the abuse that she thought, that she knew, was at the center of the case. It was the truth, but he wouldn't go near it.

She bridled, but kept her mouth shut.

It took Miranda less than a half hour to establish that something very terrible had happened at the Gardner residence shortly after Christmas 1994. Three witnesses from the Saugerties police department described, in rapid succession, the call to headquarters, the response, and the body in the trunk.

Dan Gaffney's cross-examination of the witnesses was also quick; there wasn't much worth contesting.

The first day of the trial ended there, crime estab-

lished, but James Evans not yet directly fingered—
except by his own lawyer.

Miranda took care of that the next morning, calling
as his first witness Kathy Gardner. He started slowly,
seeming almost afraid that he might hurt her with his
questions. But any such fears were quickly dispelled.
The girl spoke of the murder as directly and completely
as she had with Investigator Costello more than two
years before. The nervous shake in her voice faded as
she recalled her grandmother falling to her knees in
James' grip.

"She started to change colors," Kathy told Miranda.
"She couldn't move. Then Wendy brought me upstairs
and started singing 'Jingle Bells' or something."

Who was it whom she had seen come to the house
that night? Who was it who had slid his hands around
the woman who had raised her?

Kathy pointed at James Evans as Miranda waited for
an answer. An almost inaudible sob fell from her lips.

James, at the defense table, concentrated on a pad,
trying to avoid the gaze of everyone in the room.

Miranda had the girl continue. She told how she had
been threatened with death herself, then recounted the
shopping spree at the mall and the general partying
that had followed Betty Gardner's death. She talked
about hearing her sister's groans downstairs a few hours
after the murder, when James and Wendy were having
sex.

The jurors listened intently, some of their faces visibly
pained. Kathy Gardner testified for nearly twenty-five
minutes under Miranda's gentle prodding. Gaffney took
a breath when the assistant DA was done, then got up
and proceeded with a ginger cross-examination. His
emphasis was on the animosity between the grand-

mother and the two young lovers, but he knew there was little he could do with the witness that would impress the jurors. After about twenty minutes or so of questions, he sat back down at the table next to Evans, who had been endeavoring to keep his eyes focused on the table during the entire ordeal.

Mike Miranda had a full day and a half worth of testimony left to present, all necessary to establish the legal and technical elements of the case, but from a psychological point of view, it was all just piling on. Kathy Gardner's testimony not only showed how heartless the murder had been, but it proved the two killers had enjoyed themselves royally afterwards. There was no trace of distress, emotional or otherwise. If any member of the jury had been inclined to disbelieve Dan Gaffney's admission at the start of the trial that James Evans had committed the deed, they didn't now.

Friday afternoon, July 19, Miranda called his last witness. Judge Bruhn recessed court for the weekend. While Miranda had not yet officially rested his case, it was obvious that barring unforeseen circumstances, he would do so first thing Monday morning.

Gaffney went home feeling somewhat confident. As bad as Kathy Gardner's testimony had been, there were no surprises in it. The lawyer might even have managed to plant a few hints of the situation at the Gardner home. In any event, his opening statement, which had had a visible impact, would still be fresh in jurors' minds when court resumed next week.

Dr. Sabot would be ready Monday. They'd work through his testimony and Evans would have a good shot at the reduced charge.

Miranda, meanwhile, could hardly contain his excitement. Gaffney was obviously going to focus everything on his psychiatrist. While word was spreading in the DA's office about the planned ambush, it hadn't reached the defense attorney.

26

"You lied to this jury"

July 22, 1996

Things started slowly Monday morning. The trial didn't get underway until after eleven o'clock. The small courtroom was even more crowded than normal. Dan Gaffney noticed that some of the seats behind him were filled with members of the DA's office, who ordinarily had better things to do than take mental notes at a colleague's trial, especially on the day the defense opened its case. But so be it. He reviewed his game plan one more time, waiting for his turn to open his case.

"If you believe the credible evidence my witness has presented," he would tell the jury, "even so little as fifty percent, then you have to go with emotional disturbance."

Judge Bruhn, announced into court by his mustachioed clerk Charles "Chuck" Roach, sat down at the simple wooden bench in the front of the room. He gaveled the court into session.

Mike Miranda, as expected, completed the formality of resting the prosecution's case. An observer in the back thought he looked like he needed a cigarette.

Gaffney shifted into gear, unconsciously straightening his suit as he called his first witness, Dr. Theodore J. Sabot, licensed psychiatrist in the state of New York, to the witness stand.

Technically, expert witnesses must present their credentials before they testify, establishing the legal grounds that they are, indeed, experts. In practice, many of the experts who testify are well-known not only to the side calling them, but to the other side and the judge as well. In the interests of brevity, it is usual in Ulster County and elsewhere for both sides to waive a lengthy reading of credits, resumés, and the like into the record. But this morning Miranda shot to his feet and asked, just for form's sake, that Sabot's qualifications be added to the record. Almost apologetically, he suggested that the good doctor had not appeared in court here before, and the People just wanted the i's dotted and t's crossed.

Gaffney had no problem with that. His expert answered some routine questions about his schooling and experience, establishing his expertise beyond the shadow of a doubt, for the record. When he was done, the defense case began in earnest.

James Evans, sitting at the defense table, watched as his attorney began drawing out the facts of his early upbringing from the psychiatrist. He'd had some experience with shrinks. This one, who'd spent considerable time with him in Gaffney's office, at least seemed to be trying to help him.

Sabot spoke mostly in plain language, developing the themes he had laid out in his report. He looked thoroughly professional, comfortable, perhaps even a little arrogant in the way that specialists sometimes do when talking to laymen. But when he called James "severely depressed" he was able to give solid evidence of his finding, talking about weight loss and sleepless nights. It was not surprising that Evans had developed a "wise-ass" attitude in light of his upbringing and the constant fighting, Sabot told the jurors. The psychiatrist then explained how the romance between James and Wendy had been the one bright spot in James' bleak life.

Sabot even recounted the murder, saying that Evans had told him he "got her into a headlock to protect himself and to try to keep her away from Wendy." The murder, he contended, was unplanned, a bad situation that just escalated out of hand. "Strangling is not my style," he remembered the defendant telling him. "If I wanted to kill her, I could have just snapped her neck."

Having the psychiatrist on the stand was infinitely better than having James Evans up there, Gaffney thought. Miranda would have badgered the hell out of the kid on cross-examination. From a tactical point of view, the defense attorney was having his client give his side of the story without exposing himself to the prosecution's inevitable slashing. The psychiatrist was hitting a grand slam for the defense.

Aside from a short break, Dr. Sabot stayed on the stand for nearly two hours, presenting what Gaffney felt was a textbook justification for emotional disturbance. James Evans had not intended to kill, but had acted to defend the only love he had ever known. He had been conditioned by years of emotional, institutional, and physical abuse to see violence as the answer to any threat, any problem.

To use the formal language of Sabot's in-depth report, James Evans was "a youngster, chronically depressed and despairing, caught in a tragic relationship where he saw himself as the protector and savior of an abused girl who depended upon him, with a long history of exposure to domestic violence, [who] was suddenly put in a position where, faced with what he perceived to be a physical threat to his cherished girlfriend, suddenly exploded into a defensive but deadly act of violence."

"No further questions," Gaffney announced, walking back to the defense table. It was five minutes after one. The judge adjourned for lunch.

Miranda came off a bit like famed television detective Columbo as he began his cross-examination a little after two. He wanted to know about the doctor's background again. Sabot's tone was a cross between mild impatience and outright arrogance, as if he were instructing an errant child once more that he must clear his plate before dessert.

When he had studied Sabot's curriculum vitae, Miranda had realized that the psychiatrist had covered his California prison-release time by saying he had been in private practice on Long Island. An artful omission on paper, perhaps, but it was a hole the prosecutor could drive a dump truck through.

And he was about to.

"You have no bias against the district attorney's office, do you?" asked Miranda, seemingly in response to the psychiatrist's manner.

"Not so far," joked the psychiatrist.

The audience in the courtroom laughed.

"I promise you, you will," Miranda replied. The laughter died away as he began peppering Sabot with the questions he had relished now for three weeks.

"You lied to this jury, did you not?" he demanded, pushing Sabot for details about what he was really doing during the eighties, demanding to know if he had ever been convicted of a felony, questioning every bit of what a few hours ago had seemed the most mundane part of Sabot's testimony.

Dan Gaffney was horrified, unsure where the prosecution was going. Miranda's conduct seemed unusual, even unprofessional. He rose to object.

Miranda reached across the table and slid a copy of the California notice of conviction to him. The defense attorney slid back in his seat, dumbfounded, listening as Miranda arrived at the revelation that the defense's star witness was a criminal.

"I don't know too much," whispered James, "but this isn't too good for me, is it?"

"No," Gaffney told him.

The doctor dutifully answered the questions put to him, volunteering that he had done a stupid thing and noting that he had indeed pled guilty to felony charges brought against him. He corrected some of Miranda's information—he had only been convicted of filing $108,000 in false claims, not the $300,000 the prosecutor alleged.

The conviction had not been hidden from any of his employers, Sabot continued.

"I'm not saying you were trying to hide it from anyone

else but this jury," Miranda responded, pushing along to ask Sabot why he hadn't included it when speaking about his background.

"It was such a painful experience I tried to put it out of my mind," said the psychiatrist.

One or two of the jurors seemed to laugh.

Miranda eventually got around to questioning Theodore Sabot's statements about Evans, but by now they were almost irrelevant. It was well past four-thirty by the time he finished with the witness.

He couldn't resist one more flourish in what had been a prosecutor's dream cross-examination.

"If you were sitting in the jury box listening to your own testimony, would you believe it?"

"Objection!" shouted Gaffney.

"I don't need an answer," said Miranda, sitting.

Dan Gaffney, desperate now that his case had been indirectly but thoroughly shattered, asked the psychiatrist on redirect whether his felony conviction influenced his opinion about James Evans. Not surprisingly, Sabot answered no. With the jury out of the room, the attorney as much admitted to the judge that he had already blown the case and asked for a mistrial. It was not his client's fault, he argued, that the one witness who could help him turned out to be a felon.

"I don't see how this jury, after learning he has a prior felony record, can be fair and impartial in their evaluation of his testimony," Gaffney pleaded. "James Evans has no money and is entitled to the best defense, and I have not provided that to him."

Bruhn demurred. The felony conviction might affect the jury, he said, but then again it might not. In any event, he found no grounds for a mistrial. The trial would resume tomorrow, as scheduled.

Gaffney frowned, preparing to face the reporters outside the courtroom, whose questions this warm summer afternoon were sure to be hotter than the weather.

27

A sociopath

Dan Gaffney contemplated several moves, but his options had been severely limited by his original strategy to build his case around his single expert witness. He considered putting James on the stand and having the young man tell his story in his own words. It might be a way of restoring the jury's impression of his poor upbringing and the state of his mind.

But it was a risky way to go. Gaffney needed no reminder of Miranda's ability to tear up a witness on cross-examination; he had just had a rather graphic demonstration. Undoubtedly, the assistant district attorney had done an even better job preparing for Evans, and was licking his chops at the prospect.

The defense attorney decided that Evans' best chance was on appeal. The lawyer would take the highly unusual step of declaring the job of defending James incompetent, based on his choice of expert witness. The best way to do that was to shut down right away. By not presenting other witnesses, he wouldn't muddy the waters. In effect, he was hoping that the appeals court would look at the case and say, boy, this kid had such a lousy lawyer we have to give him another shot.

Not exactly Dan Gaffney's proudest moment at the bar. Even if the odds in the case had been greatly stacked against his client, it was still a hell of a way to lose, especially since he was convinced the kid deserved better. It was no consolation that no other defense attorney in the state would have bothered to ask a potential expert witness if he had a felony conviction.

They would from now on.

Miranda was ready when Gaffney rested the defense as soon as the trial resumed Tuesday. He wasn't gloating, exactly, but he sure as hell was smiling.

In case the jury was tempted to disregard Sabot's felony conviction, or the rest of Miranda's cross-examination, the prosecutor called his own expert, Dr. Kevin Smith, as a rebuttal witness. Smith, one of the few psychological experts DA Mike Kavanagh liked and felt knew what he was talking about, often testified in cases on behalf of the prosecution. The head of the psychiatric unit at the local hospital, Smith came across as a competent, knowledgeable witness. Miranda had held him back for the *coup de grace*.

The doctor testified that he had met with James Evans for a total of four hours in two sessions earlier in the month. James, he said, had told two different stories about the murder. In the first, he said he didn't remember the killing at all; in the second, he describing having his hands around Mrs. Gardner's neck when Wendy yelled, "Just do it!" and dragged Kathy upstairs. It was the second version that Smith believed was true.

"He said he had not actually been truthful with me or with anyone else," Smith told Miranda when he was asked about his second session with the defendant. "He was afraid to, without his attorney's permission."

Even Evans' second version of the murder story was, at best, incomplete. It left out the kite string and inaccurately portrayed the final cause of death. But Miranda— and Gaffney, for that matter—didn't point this out.

"He described it as a sleeper hold, which cuts off blood to the brain so a person passes out," said Smith. "Wendy yelled out, 'Just do it.' He remembers Kathy screaming quite a bit." The psychiatrist paused momentarily. "While he's performing this procedure, [Betty Gardner] took a last single exhalation of her breath, and he even gave a demonstration of what that's like."

Dr. Smith also claimed that Evans told him he hadn't been truthful with the defense psychiatrist.

Much of what Smith said about his interviews with Evans would be familiar to anyone who had heard Dr. Sabot's initial testimony or read his detailed report. The defense psychiatrist had also encountered resistance at first and finally gotten a more accurate account of the murder, one that included the murder weapon. But the real difference was in the prosecution psychiatrist's interpretation. He told the jurors that James Evans was not suffering from extreme emotional disturbance. Instead, as had the earlier therapists Sabot himself had cited, Smith diagnosed Evans as having a conduct disorder—he was simply anti-social, or a sociopath.

Bad, yes. Evil, sure. But that didn't get him off the

hook for murder. Quite the contrary. Smith would later say he was convinced the young man would kill again, if given the chance.

Dan Gaffney's cross-examination lasted a half hour, but the air had gone out of him and his case. The high point came when the defense attorney asked, "You haven't been convicted of any crime, have you?"

"No," said Dr. Smith.

"That's refreshing," cracked the lawyer, convulsing the jury with sympathetic laughter.

They weren't sympathetic toward his client when deliberations began at noon the next day. At first, one or two jurors wanted Sabot's testimony read back to them, along with Smith's. But then they changed their minds; a note was sent out to the judge requesting Kathy's testimony.

Shortly after 8 P.M., July 24, the eight men and four women filed back into the wood-paneled courtroom in the historic building on Wall Street and announced that they had reached a verdict.

James Evans was asked to stand. Stoop-shouldered, hands dangling free at the side of his blue shirt and dark pants, he rose slowly, then faced them as the verdict was read.

Guilty of murder in the second degree. Not manslaughter.

Opinions were split afterward on whether or not the psychiatrist's felony conviction had truly affected the jurors. Many observers believed that it had not, and pointed to the request for the read-back as proof that his analysis was taken seriously. Others, especially people like Gaffney associated with the defense, believed it was everything.

The judge set August 22 for sentencing. The deputies moved in. No one outside the family had really believed James Evans was innocent; they no longer had to pretend.

"I love you, James," called his sister Donna as he was led from the courtroom.

If this is justice, they can blow the whole world up, thought his mother as she walked sadly from the courtroom.

Betty Gardner's sisters Rose and June, who'd come to every session, left as quietly as possible, rejoicing to themselves that justice had been done.

28

Coda

A strange coda remained to be played out at James Evans' sentencing hearing the following month. For when the judge started the proceeding, Dan Gaffney rose and asked permission to approach the bench.

"It has come to my attention from an impeccable source that there is a most definite question as to whether or not there was jury misconduct in regards to Mr. Evans' trial," the lawyer declared grandiloquently. "There is a question to the integrity of certain answers given by a juror during voir dire."

The impeccable source had apparently been the district attorney's office, which had found, as the result of some routine paperwork involving a pistol permit, that one of the jurors who convicted Evans had been facing a charge of assaulting his daughter in a family dispute at the time. As Miranda later explained it in a lengthy filing, the misdemeanor charge had been filed in a town court by the state police but not properly followed up. On his questionnaire, the juror left the line asking if he had had any dealings with the police or DA blank.

The juror signed a statement swearing that he believed the charge had been dropped, and didn't realize he had what at least gave the appearance of a conflict of interest. He also swore that he had not been biased in any way, or been offered any favors in connection with either case.

Miranda argued somewhat incredibly that it was the prosecution and not the defense that stood to be harmed by the juror. In any event, there was no evidence that the man had done anything to take advantage of the situation or that the jury or its deliberations had been tampered with in any way. The assault charge was apparently later dropped or dismissed in the local court.

Though Bruhn's first action was to slap a gag order on the defense and prosecution—the first of his career, he noted—the judge eventually found that nothing untoward had happened and sentenced James Evans, to the maximum, nine years to life.

Dan Gaffney stewed about Sabot all through the summer. He also filed a two-page affirmation with the court saying that his failure to "ask Dr. Theodore J. Sabot if he had been previously convicted of a crime" had led directly to the failure of the jury to find James Evans guilty of the lesser charge.

An appeal was filed on Evans' behalf with the state's Third Judicial Department Appellate Division. In essence, it alleged that incompetent counsel, i.e. Gaff-

ney's failure to ask Sabot about the felony, was responsible for his conviction. Therefore, the conviction should
be overturned.

The appeal was expected to be perfected sometime
during or after the spring of 1998, after this book was
written.

James Evans' appeals attorney, Carl J. Silverstein,
believes there may be some solid grounds for overturn-
ing the conviction, though he notes the case is unusual.
In his opinion, the district attorney's office may have
been ethically obligated to inform the defense of Sabot's
conviction, since the psychiatrist's testimony amounted
to such a major portion of the defense case.

Mike Kavanagh admitted later that he would have felt
personally obliged to tell Gaffney about the witness;
they'd been old friends. But he defended his assistants'
decision, and said in any event the psychiatrist's credibility wouldn't have made much difference to the final
outcome. Emotional disturbance as a defense works only
when a jury wants to acquit someone, he said, and that
wasn't the case here.

As for the appeal, Kavanagh thought it would never
fly. His old friend had too good a record in Ulster
County Court to get away with calling himself a bust as
an attorney.

Following his sentencing, the seventeen-year-old James
Evans was first assigned to a DFY facility in Dutchess
County near Connecticut. While in theory the youth
detention center is supposed to shield youngsters from
the harsher conditions, and inmates, found in adult

prisons, a newspaper report not connected with the case but published around the same time called the center one of the most dangerous places in the state's entire corrections establishment.

According to his family, Evans has received no counseling there, but records show he has done well in his high school equivalency classes.

VII

SHE WORE A FLOWERED DRESS

29

From yadas to yahoos

Late Fall 1996

The ancient stairs groaned as Jeremiah Flaherty—Jerry to his friends, enemies, and most clients—charged up to his office, escaping the damp, mountainside cold. He was in a typical Flaherty mood: unsatisfied, jumbling a dozen things at once in his head, vaguely annoyed that he wasn't going to spend the afternoon beating somebody up in court.

Or watching his son and the other local kids play baseball.

He poked his head into his reception area, greeting the "girls" with a sound something like a bear makes when woken in the middle of hibernation. With nothing pressing to tell their boss, the two assistants let him grumble on a minute, then rolled their eyes at each other as the attorney disappeared across the hall into his office.

Flaherty closed the door behind him. Glancing briefly at the mountain of files on the ornate green leather bench in front of his desk, he slid into his brown leather chair. Swiveling as he sifted through the mail, he came across the report from Dr. Kevin Smith on Wendy Gardner. He ran a thick, pink finger through his blown-back white hair before starting to read it.

A few months before, it had looked like the district attorney was going to offer a plea bargain, allowing Gardner to plead guilty to manslaughter. Flaherty's heart had jumped—the charge would mean she would be sentenced by family court, and if she got the sentence he expected, she would be out practically on time already served.

At the time, the DA's office apparently hadn't realized that. Then someone had researched the law. And either because of that or because of an outcry from the public and within Kavanagh's office, the charge remained murder.

Frowning, Flaherty swung around in his seat and began reading through Smith's report, mumbling to himself as he went. The psychiatrist was the prosecution's expert. In not so many words he could be expected to declare Flaherty's client one notch below Lizzie Borden in the great panoply of female criminals.

Except, he didn't.

As the lawyer continued, his mumbles turned from yadas to yahoos. Dr. Smith, the prosecution's expert, the man who had nailed home the case against James Evans, said Wendy Gardner was suffering from emotional disturbance and ought to get off with manslaughter, not murder.

Really?

Flaherty reread the report, seriously this time, without the mumbling. Sometimes these experts couldn't be trusted.

The attorney had been in the audience the previous July when Dan Gaffney had put Dr. Sabot on the stand. He had himself been thinking of an emotional disturbance defense, and he was impressed with Sabot's thoroughness.

Other appointments had kept Flaherty from seeing Mike Miranda's shining moment that afternoon, though he'd gotten all the gory details soon enough. In a way, it was a relief that Gaffney's play had failed and James Evans had been convicted of murder. Flaherty would have a villain, who could be invoked in countless ways during Wendy's trial, a ghost in chains rattling on cue.

Still, if truth be told, Jerry Flaherty's hand wasn't a very strong one. Miranda would play Gardner's taped confession for the jury and that might just blow him away right there. It wasn't just because it laid out her involvement in the murder—that was so clear from other evidence that his best strategy was probably going to be the emotional disturbance play anyway. But that angle required a sympathetic response from the jury, and the tape wouldn't provoke one.

Quite the contrary. The voice on it was very cold. The girl came off very, very badly, and though he'd masterfully stage-managed her public image until now, there was no getting around that tape.

Like just about everyone else who met her, the lawyer liked Wendy Gardner; he saw the kid in her, down under the wall she put up, beyond the withdrawal that to him was a sure symptom of a horribly difficult early life. She was a smart kid, though that wasn't necessarily an asset.

Flaherty once described the problem with defending smart people to a visitor. Essentially, it came down to talking too much. Someone who was smart and conscientious, as he thought Wendy was, tended to try to explain everything. They would talk and talk, and eventually that got them into trouble. Much better, the veteran defense lawyer felt, to have a dumb client who just said yes or no when asked a question. They didn't get themselves in trouble.

And another thing. Gardner tried too hard to make a good impression sometimes. She'd shown up for a meeting once with her hair in corn rows, not exactly the innocent little girl image her attorney wanted to project. When Flaherty asked, in his red-faced apocalyptic style, why she had done her hair like a ghetto kid, she said all of the other girls at the detention center told her it would go over big with the court.

"Were they black?" Flaherty asked.

The girl nodded. She never wore her hair that way again.

Wendy Gardner did well in her classes at the detention center, and at least one of the counselors later called her a model prisoner. She was quiet and tended to keep to herself.

She was much the same with Flaherty, but that wasn't an asset for a lawyer trying to prepare a defense. She had a solid wall around her emotions, and it made her come off cold.

He'd gotten her to lower that wall right here, in this office, on the little chair near his desk, though only after a year and a half of meeting with her. It had begun with a silly story, her retelling some juvenile incident in the neighborhood, James throwing pears and a neighbor calling the police. The details were trivial, but her laugh wasn't—a real, honest laugh, opening her up, making her a little girl, not a cold-blooded murder defendant.

If he could show that to a jury, his case would be won. Because from there it was hardly a leap to conclude that James Evans, a neighborhood bully who had already been declared a sociopath and a murderer in a court of law, had gotten her under his sway and forced her to help kill her grandmother. Sure, Wendy had gone along; her mind had been twisted the way a kidnap victim's was. It was Patty Hearst all over again, the Stockholm Syndrome played out in little old Saugerties. James Evans was the killer here; Wendy Gardner was just the tool for his pleasure, as much a means to an end as the kite string had been.

And now Dr. Smith agreed. The prosecution's own expert believed, in his professional, unbiased opinion, that Wendy Gardner had been so completely under the sway of the bully of Barclay Heights she would go along with anything he suggested.

Flaherty rocked back and forth his chair. He almost wished the case started today. The first thing he had to do was call Smith and see if he would testify—for the defense.

Kevin Smith agreed. But even with him on his side, Flaherty realized there were several problems with the case and the emotional disturbance strategy.

The concept itself would be difficult if not impossible for laymen to understand. In James Evans' case, Judge Bruhn's instructions to the jury ran several single-spaced pages. And even if the jurors understood it, they might be tempted to render a judgment based on their emotions rather than complicated legal standards. If Mike Miranda had to worry about jury nullification—the fancy way of saying that jurors in their gut felt sorry for a defendant and so let him or her off—Flaherty and other defense attorneys had to worry about the opposite. Jurors in Ulster tended to be conservative, and in this case would not only have the image of a kindly grandmother in front of them, courtesy of the prosecutor, but would have ample opportunity to interpret his client at her very worst, courtesy of an assortment of witnesses as well as the taped confession. The prosecution would be doing everything in its power to portray Gardner as a calculating, out-of-control, sex-crazed youth who had told investigators she had asked her boyfriend to murder her grandma. Emotions, not fine points of the law, might prevail.

Because emotional disturbance was a legal issue, Jerry Flaherty finally decided that he would be better off presenting it to someone who was not only familiar with the concept but had recently studied it in depth—Judge Bruhn himself. By waiving a jury trial, the defense attorney would be making an unusual move. Though it is an option in New York State, few murder cases are decided by a judge alone. Nonetheless, if the case could be held to narrow legal issues, Flaherty felt that Dr. Smith's report would tip it in Gardner's favor, especially since Bruhn would be well aware of Smith's reputation and the fact that he had been called into the case by the prosecution.

There was only one problem with that strategy.

Wendy didn't like it. She wanted a jury trial. So did her father. So did Lisa Beth Older, another lawyer Buzz

Gardner had retained on a pro bono basis to serve as co-counsel.

And to make matters worse, Wendy Gardner wanted to testify on her own behalf in court.

30

Twelve minds

February, 1997

A Sawzall rattled in the background as Jerry Flaherty and Lisa Beth Older began to discuss the situation with Wendy Gardner in a small holding room in the old courthouse. Renovation work was going on all around them and the small room was like a tiny oasis in a sea of chaos. Judge Bruhn was holding preliminary hearings on Gardner's trial a few rooms away. Flaherty had decided this morning it was now or never in his bid to convince Wendy to waive the jury.

The lawyer, his red-tinged mustache twitching at the corners, calmly laid out the case for a judge-only trial. The girl had come a long way since their first meetings, when Flaherty would explain something, ask if she understood, get a nod, and then field a series of questions that revealed the thirteen-year-old hadn't gotten the point at all. Now fifteen, Gardner listened to the arguments about the difficulty of explaining the legal issue to the jury. She turned to her other lawyer, and saw that she too was agreeing.

Lisa Beth Older did not have as much experience as Jerry Flaherty. Nonetheless, she had represented clients in both county and family courts, and had worked with Flaherty on a previous murder case. In fact, it had been through him that she first met Wendy Gardner and her father, though the two lawyers had subsequently fallen out over strategy—this point in particular.

The Woodstock-area lawyer felt a particular affinity to Wendy. Older had run away from home as a youngster, and while there were no exact parallels in their life stories, she felt a connection with the girl that lawyers seldom feel for clients. Some observers, most notably members of the district attorney's office, believed that Older had gotten herself involved in the case because she sensed there was publicity value. Older had, in fact, told a local newspaper reporter that she discussed the case with Johnnie Cochran and that the famous lawyer had expressed an interest in doing a television show on it for *Court TV*. But Older saw her involvement as one more chance to champion the rights of the less fortunate, especially when they were troubled young women. She liked to point out that she had done that her entire life, even serving as a girls' club director in California. In any event, there was never much public focus on her role in connection with the trial. If anything, her advice against waiving a jury trial was conventional, from a legal point of view.

Though she had argued against it until now, this cold February morning, Lisa Beth Older was convinced by

Flaherty's arguments, and she agreed as long as Gardner did.

And Gardner did.

Flaherty suppressed any surprise he felt and quickly marched back before Judge Bruhn. He announced in his West Side accent that his client had reached a decision: she wanted to waive her right to a jury trial.

Bruhn was silent for a moment as he considered the situation. His duty was clear; he had to determine if Flaherty's young client had truly reached this decision and understood what it meant. And so he began a patient voir dire, questioning Wendy Gardner about what she wanted to do and explaining what her options were.

It wasn't long before she told the judge that, now that she truly considered it, she did want a jury trial.

Twelve minds were better than one.

If Bruhn, who possessed a wry sense of humor, smiled at the unconscious and unintended put-down, it never made it to the official records.

Flaherty was disappointed, to put it mildly, but he had had reversals before. There was no way to go against what his client wanted, so he moved on, preparing to fight in an environment he enjoyed.

Older fell back to her original belief that it would be easier to win the sympathy of the jury than the judge. She also started preparing for her questioning of Gardner on the stand.

There would be some disagreement after the trial as to exactly who had advocated what tactic when and why. To some extent, the defense attorneys' differences may have been the result of an ego clash, as neither had a personality that could be likened to milquetoast.

Older said firmly that she never wanted Gardner to testify, but that once she decided to, she tried to prep her as best she could. Flaherty tended to view Older more as a hindrance than a help, certainly after the fact. He implied that had the other attorney not been there, he might have been able to talk Wendy, and more importantly, her father Buzz, who was a powerful influence on her, into both waiving a jury and not testifying on her own behalf. Both decisions, he felt, were serious mistakes that handicapped his defense.

With the trial ready to start, Bruhn ruled that Gardner's taped confession, along with some other evidence gathered by the police, was admissible in court. The tape was the most important, and the judge found that Wendy had been advised of her rights and that her father had been present, points clearly revealed at the beginning of the tape.

The plea bargain that the district attorney had floated the year before was no longer even talked about.

Better to let twelve people decide the verdict, said Mike Kavanaugh, when asked about it by the press.

With the trial about to begin, the defense made one more move to position its client's image in the public eye: Wendy Gardner was made available to the local media for interviews. She made a good impression.

Times Herald Record reporter John Milgrim had told Mike Miranda that he couldn't understand why there was even a trial, since Dr. Smith had recommended for the lesser trial. His story shaded completely toward Gardner's version of events, saying at one point that Wendy had put her faith in James Evans, only to see him kill her grandmother.

The story sympathetically laid out the general direction Jerry Flaherty's case would take, and included the fact that Gardner's mother had recently died of complications apparently related to AIDS. It also noted that her father had attended most court appearances.

Wendy, who spoke to Milgrim by phone while Flaherty was by her side, told the reporter that she believed people were basically good, and that because of that, they would find her guilty of the lesser charge. She talked briefly about the upcoming trial, admitting that she was worried about what would happen. She also said that she still loved her sister, though she expected her to take the stand and testify against her.

The interview with Cynthia Werthamer came in person during a break in the trial and ran in the *Kingston Freeman* the day after Milgrim's appeared. Much more neutral in tone, the story led with the fact that Wendy Gardner claimed she didn't love James Evans, and probably never had.

Now that she had spoken to a lot of psychiatrists, the teenager told the reporter, she realized that what she was feeling wasn't love.

Gardner also told Werthamer how much she loved her sister, who had been called to testify the same day as the interview. Cynthia Werthamer's shorter story was a sidebar to a larger account covering Kathy's testimony. Where John Milgrim had emphasized the psychiatrist's recommendations, Werthamer mentioned that the teenager was wearing a demure flower-print dress for the opening of the trial, rather than the jeans or miniskirt she had worn to court for the pre-trial hearings. It was an observation that many watching the trial had made, with snickers of contempt at the obviousness of the ploy.

When the reporter asked about that during the interview, Older, who had paid for Wendy's court outfit out of her own pocket, quickly came to Gardner's defense, saying that she had chosen the clothes herself and not because they would have any particular effect on the jury.

31

"I want to kill her"

February 13-14, 1997

On the morning of February 13, Gweneviere "Wendy" Gardner entered the small, temporary courtroom in the Ulster County Courthouse wearing an ankle-length, flower-print dress. A blue crucifix and rosary beads hung around her neck. The beads were eerily reminiscent of a set that had swung from the mirror of her grandmother's car before her murder, though few if any of those cramming into the room knew that.

A host of news organizations had arranged to cover the trial, and their reporters filled many of the limited seats. A few of Wendy's relatives were also there, along with a smattering of neighbors, other acquaintances, and a handful of the curious, including a few lawyers. For some reason, there seemed more immediate interest in Wendy's trial than in James Evans'. A lot of people wondered why Betty Gardner had died, and they looked for this proceeding to answer the question. One veteran newsman commented later that the people in Saugerties hadn't reacted with outrage because of the family circumstances. They had decided the people involved were basically dysfunctional, and while deeply troubled by the killing, in a way they could understand it. But if that were true, the feeling didn't carry to the world at large or even to the rest of the county. People on the street were buzzing about the case, and the word on their lips was "Why?"

Why did Betty Gardner have to die?

Sitting at the prosecutor's table, Mike Miranda pondered the question himself. While he felt he had a tremendous case, and was by now as expert in its nuances as anyone, he could not satisfactorily answer the question. It would gnaw at him as the trial proceeded.

Miranda's attitude toward Wendy Gardner fluctuated. There was no question in his mind that she was guilty; most days he thought she was more culpable than Evans. He looked at her now in the demure dress and practically snapped, "Little Boo Peep," out loud. Though dressing up defendants was one of the oldest tricks in the book, this seemed so outrageous it would probably backfire. It must be Older's doing, he thought, not Flaherty's.

But there was also a gnawing at the back of Miranda's mind, a nagging emotion if not of doubt, maybe of compassion. James Evans had been older, and he had had trouble with the law before. Wendy had been barely thirteen.

Did that make her innocent?

Hardly.

But did it mitigate in her favor?

No, the attorney decided, she had committed murder and it was his job to prosecute her. She was at least as guilty as Evans was. The community wanted justice, and it was his job to deliver it.

Still, something kept tugging at him as the trial got under way. There was something about Wendy Gardner. During one of the earlier hearings in the judge's chamber, Miranda had passed her a piece of candy from the jar the judge kept on his desk. He could have been giving a piece of candy to one of his own girls.

Having won once with the case against James Evans, the assistant district attorney planned on following the same game plan, calling mostly the same witnesses in essentially the same order. The difference the second time around was mostly in emphasis and brevity. From his opening statement to his questioning of the witnesses, Miranda's pace was sharp and to the point. In rapid succession, he called three police witnesses, establishing the facts of the crime.

Jerry Flaherty had anticipated that Miranda would find it a bit more difficult to get excited the second time around, but he found no obvious flaws in the attorney's style or manner, much less the way he was proceeding. If Miranda was bored, he sure wasn't showing it.

The defense team's cross-examinations the first day, all conducted by the veteran Flaherty, were brief. There was little to be gained belaboring the obvious. By 12:30, Judge Bruhn was declaring a recess for lunch.

When court reconvened an hour and a half later, Miranda rose and called Kathy Gardner to the stand.

He watched her walk to the stand in her brown sweater and beige skirt, confident even though she was about to face her sister for the first time in court. She took the oath and sat in the witness stand. The district attorney fell right into his questioning.

Tears had already formed in Wendy's eyes. She held her gaze at her sister, listening as the younger girl began recounting what had happened the night of December 28, 1994.

"Do you see her now?" Miranda asked, the time-worn prosecutor's line to show the jury exactly whom a witness was accusing of murder.

Kathy Gardner pointed. "She's sitting there between those two lawyers," she answered, turning away as she continued to describe how Wendy had smashed her head against the wall, then held her down so she couldn't escape.

For about a half hour more, Kathy talked about the killing and its aftermath, repeating the story she had told James Evans' jury. Miranda moved through it easily, sympathetically, bringing out the highlights as he noted to himself that the jury's attention was riveted on his witness. Then he turned her over to Flaherty.

Flaherty knew Kathy Gardner was a credible, persuasive witness. He was counting on that. His cross-examination ignored, for the most part, what she had said about the murder. He was interested in something else. The lawyer began recalling incidents when Wendy had been punished. Was there a time when a penny was dropped into a radiator?

Yes, said Kathy.

Did she recall what her grandmother had done?

"She might have smacked her across the face for stealing something from me."

In fact, Kathy did recall that her grandmother punished the girls, using a paddle and a fly swatter.

"The paddle didn't hurt very much," she added. "And the fly swatter just stung sometimes."

Flaherty moved on, asking about the girls' father. Kathy said that he often argued with her grandmother, drank her liquor, visited only occasionally.

He had also claimed to have been arguing with his own father when he died.

Flaherty let it all sink in as he walked back to the defense table. As damaging as Kathy Gardner's direct testimony against her sister was, he had been able to use the prosecution's witness to lay the groundwork for his own defense.

Back at the table, Wendy choked back a sob and watched as her sister was dismissed.

Contrary to popular opinion, there are seldom surprises at a murder trial. The rules of court procedure strongly mitigate against the dramatic entrances and hearty breakdowns so common in the movies and old dramas like *Perry Mason*. This case was not an exception. Both the prosecution and defense were well aware of each other's witnesses and probably could have predicted with reasonable certainty the exact questions each would ask. And so the next day began more or less routinely, with Miranda calling Dr. Jeffrey Hubbard to the stand to testify about how Mrs. Gardner had died. Hubbard talked about the effects of ligature strangulation on a human body.

Suddenly, Wendy Gardner jumped up from her chair and began running toward the door, her hands to her mouth. Two jail guards followed her inside a bathroom, where she was throwing up.

For weeks, Jerry Flaherty had toyed with the idea of somehow getting James Evans on the stand. The lawyer was convinced that if the jurors saw his moody anger explode, they would believe Wendy Gardner had been frightened enough to go along with anything, even murder.

But it was a risky play, even if James agreed to talk, which he was not obligated to do. If the teenager decided to say Wendy had killed her grandmother, not him, that could be dealt with. There was all sorts of testimony to the contrary, and it would be child's play for the experienced defense attorney to sweat Evans on the stand. But if he decided instead to say that Wendy had planned it, if rather than playing the tough guy he somehow broke down on the stand, confessing the murder and saying he wished he'd never listened to her, the defense case would sink faster than the *Titanic*.

Flaherty went back and forth, trying to figure out what James Evans would do. Some of his instincts said James would go nuts; some said he wouldn't. Part of the difficulty was the fact that the former lovers hadn't been together now for more than two years. Wendy had just told a reporter she didn't love him and never had. What was James feeling?

It wasn't a straight-ahead call for legal reasons as well. Evans' case was under appeal; if it were overturned, anything he said here might be used against him. A lawyer assigned to Evans strongly advised against his testifying, urging him to take the Fifth Amendment if called. In fact, it was possible that legal maneuvering could keep him out of the courtroom entirely.

The legal question gave Flaherty an opening. He asked Bruhn to schedule a hearing on whether or not Evans could testify. Evans was driven to the courthouse Friday, waiting in silence out of the jury's sight as the case proceeded without him. Finally, the judge took advantage of a break to hold the hearing in his chambers.

The small, temporary office was dominated by a long table that sat like the stem of a T below Bruhn's desk. James sat on one side, Wendy on the other, both silent. As the legal issues were presented to the judge, Wendy gazed steadily on James; he spent most of his time looking at the table.

No dummy, Evans must have been aware that he was here because Gardner's attorneys wanted a scapegoat for the murder. A few months before he had told a psychiatrist that he still loved her. In the jumble of emotions now, he was caught between two opposing impulses: one was to help her, the other was to help himself. Recently turned eighteen, he had already spent more than two years behind bars. Even under the best of circumstances, he was headed toward a very long run in prison.

Suddenly there was silence, the lawyers temporarily out of things to say.

"I don't hate you, Wendy," said James, turning his face toward her.

Tears started to form in her eyes.

"All right, all right, I'll testify," said Evans in reaction. "I'll do it."

His whole manner had changed in the instant Wendy's tears started to flow. If he wasn't still in love, he was damn close. Anything she wanted, anything she needed, it was hers.

Flaherty put up his hand. That was the last thing he wanted the jury to see. He let the legal arguments drift away.

Later, when Evans was placed in his holding cell, someone saw him smashing his head against the wall as the lock was slammed home.

It was Valentine's Day.

Mike Miranda spent the rest of the morning and early afternoon with two state troopers, working his way toward the end of his case even though he had begun presenting it little more than twenty-four hours ago. He planned on heading off Flaherty's emotional disturbance tactic with an unimpeachable witness: Wendy Gardner herself.

The prosecution could not put the defendant on the stand. The Constitution protects everyone from incriminating themselves, and no district attorney would ever get away with calling a defendant to the stand.

But Miranda didn't intend to. Instead, he called Investigator Stan O'Dell to the front of the room. After O'Dell was seated, Miranda began asking about O'Dell's interview with the defendant on that New Year's Eve.

Then he played the tape of that interview for the jury.

The little girl's voice echoed off the low ceiling of the courtroom, soft, delicate—and as hard and cold as any convicted murderer staring at the blood dripping from his fingers:

[Grandma] said, 'No, I don't want you being there at all. You're never gonna go back there again.' And I said in my own words, 'Fuck you, bitch. I'm staying here tonight no matter what you say.' After that I hung up and I talked to James a little bit. I said, 'She's such a bitch' over and over again. . . . And then I called another time and this time she said, 'If you keep calling, I'm going to call the police.' So that put me into a rage and I got up and talked to James some more and I said, 'I want to kill her so bad.' She was making me so angry and then James goes, 'She's making me angry, too.' And then James goes, 'I love you, Wendy.' And I said, 'I'm not sure about that, James. I love you too . . . but I'm not sure what it is. . . .' I said, 'I just want to kill her.' And then [James said] 'If I kill her, will you love me?' And I said, 'Yeah, but I don't think you'll do it.' And James goes, 'You want to bet?' And um, and then I said, 'I don't know, James. . . .'

He said, 'I can get a gun,' and then I said, 'No, don't bother, we should just get it over with now, and quick so, before we change our minds.' I said, 'Yeah, why don't we chop her up?' And he said, 'Too much blood, but besides, you wouldn't want to do that, seeing someone's arm cut off, or her head chopped off or something.' And I said, 'Yeah, that's bad. Why don't we stab her?' 'Still too much blood,' [he said] and then he said, 'Why don't we snap her neck and if that doesn't work, we can try to choke her.' And I said, 'Yeah . . .'

The voice ground on, telling much the same story that Kathy Gardner had, though in a colder voice and in considerably more detail. One of the jurors bit his lip as she described the murder, how she ordered Evans to "just do it" after he grabbed Betty Gardner around the neck and waited for Wendy to recite the line they'd rehearsed.

At the defense table, Lisa Beth Older shifted nervously. She believed that much of the confession must have been suggested by the police; the girl had been in that station for hours, after all. Older felt very strongly about that. But she also could tell the confession was creaming her client.

The child on the tape recording could have been giving a book report, telling the police, and now the world, how she took her eleven-year-old sister upstairs and held her while James Evans finished choking Betty Gardner to death in the basement. She sang Christmas carols to drown out the noise "because it was Christmas and all." And she kept her little sister hostage and suggested to James, "You can fuck her instead of me."

Finally she came to the part where she and James made love with her grandmother's body lumped on the garage floor a few feet away. A strange feeling had come over her then, as if the old woman were somehow staring at them through the sheetrock with her dead eyes.

"... We woke up like a half an hour from not being tired from what we'd done. James goes, 'We gotta do it and I need your help.' So I go, 'No, no, I don't want to do it.' And he goes, 'Well I can't lift her, she's too heavy.' I go, 'Fine. I just don't want her looking at us.' And he, we went in the garage and I climbed over a body and stepped over it, and I grabbed her feet and he grabbed her by the back of the bra strap in under her shirt, and lifted her. And um, we pulled her over and she flipped over and we saw her face with the blood

dripping up the side of it and I didn't even bother
to look at her neck. I just pushed really heavily
'cause I didn't want to look at it. And, um, James
saw her feet hanging out the other side of the
trunk so he jammed them back in and I helped
'cause I didn't want to look at it. I slammed the
trunk and we walked in and he goes, 'It's done,
baby, don't cry.' And I started to cry, cry really
hard, and when we walked in I sat on the bed, and
we got undressed from getting dressed to go out
in the garage 'cause it was freezing. And I think,
if I'm right, we had sex. No, we didn't have sex
again, but we were talking and we made out. . . .

The tape went on for an hour and a half. By the time
the player snapped off, the soft faces of the jurors had
turned pale and harder than the cement quarried a few
miles north of the murder site. Even Stan O'Dell felt
goosebumps on his skin.

Outside, the sun slowly sank behind the buildings,
the afternoon slipping toward evening. Miranda had
timed it beautifully. Court recessed for a long weekend,
leaving the jurors three days to think about what they
had just heard.

32

"In combination with seduction"

February 18, 1997

Jeremiah Flaherty took a step back toward the defense table, trying to get his bearings. For the briefest moment all kinds of emotions battled inside of him, none of them very nice. He was great at thinking on his feet, it was what he did best, really, but his feet weren't thinking very fast. He felt like he was getting torpedoed, big time.

On the witness stand, Dr. Kevin Smith adjusted his glasses and waited for the next question. Though he was used to sitting in this chair, he was in an unfamiliar position. Ordinarily, he testified for the prosecution—but there was no difference, really, as far as he was concerned. He was here to render his informed opinion; one side or another, the truth was the truth.

But Flaherty wasn't feeling that way. When he'd called Smith to the witness stand a few minutes before, he'd felt confident he was unleashing his case's strongest witness. But the answers to his first few questions had hurt, not helped. Smith told the jury killing her grandmother was a game for Wendy Gardner.

The defense attorney had spent the morning calling a succession of neighbors and friends, whose testimony helped establish two key points. The first was that Wendy's grandmother was, at the minimum, a strict disciplinarian, if not outright abusive. The second was that James Evans was feared as a bully in the neighborhood. Now Dr. Smith, the man the prosecution had brought in to examine Wendy Gardner's mental state, was supposed to tie the earlier testimony together in a neat little legal knot called "emotional disturbance."

But it wasn't happening. Smith seemed, in fact, to be blaming her for the murder.

Flaherty took a breath and began rocking on his feet. Rocking on his feet kicked up his energy level. Kicking up his energy level got him rolling. As his hands jabbed at the air, he shouldered his upper body forward, asking for explanations the jury could understand, asking precisely what this eminently qualified expert could tell the jury about the distressed young woman he had interviewed on the prosecution's behalf.

And just like that, it began to flow.

"The defense mechanisms in her case were primitive, ones you'd expect to see in a seven- or eight-year-old," Smith testified. "The feelings of hatred, wanting her grandmother's death . . . for her it was a game. It was play. She never took it seriously."

Better. And then better and better.

In Smith's opinion, Gardner's childish mental state made her resolve conflict through play. All of the talk about killing her grandmother was actually a game to her, something that would never happen. Talking about it helped her resolve her inner conflicts and turmoil. Smith also believed that the talk excited James Evans. The more turned on he got, the better. In his opinion, she wasn't capable of considering the consequences.

Flaherty's mood lifted considerably as Dr. Smith portrayed Wendy Gardner as a child beaten by her strict grandmother. Smith told the jurors that she did well in school and was conscientious until she met James Evans. While the psychiatrist didn't necessarily trust everything Wendy had told him, he believed that, at a minimum, the girl legitimately thought she had been abused. In his opinion, her "emotional age" as an eight-year-old was critical. It was one of the things that kept her from forming clear judgments when she became involved with James.

"James became her only identified source of self-esteem," Smith said. Wendy would do anything James wanted to keep that self-esteem.

Though the jury didn't know it, his conclusion was an eerie mirror-image of the conclusion the defense expert had reached in the earlier trial, speaking about James.

The jurors edged toward the front of their chairs as Flaherty asked the psychiatrist about Evans, whom he had also examined. Smith said James Evans had an anti-social disorder. Flaherty got him to use the term psychopath, seemingly better than sociopath, seemingly a breath away from heartless mass murderer. People like James, said Smith, would use force and pain to get what they wanted.

Like terrorists did.

"Force and pain in combination with seduction," noted the psychiatrist.

That was why Betty Gardner had been killed. Her granddaughter was merely a pawn in the hands of a psychopath.

Sitting at his table, Mike Miranda didn't buy it. But Kevin Smith had been his witness in James Evans' trial, and would undoubtedly testify for the district attorney's office in other cases. The cross-examination had to be done gently.

Besides, he was a pretty nice guy, even if he was wrong on this.

He was wrong, wasn't he?

Flaherty wrung every ounce from the psychiatrist, who was a well-spoken, potent witness. He believed that Wendy Gardner had suffered from a single episode of major depression on the night of the murder. And as for the comment about "just do it"—well, she had said it meant showing her grandmother the Christmas presents.

When Flaherty turned Smith over to Miranda, the prosecutor managed to raise some doubt with one or two of the jurors. Psychiatry is an inexact science, he pointed out. It was more a rhetorical point than a question, though Smith, of course, had to agree. And the doctor had examined Wendy more than a year after the murder, hadn't he?

Yes, said Smith. More than a year later.

He might have asked similar questions and gotten similar answers at Evans' trial.

Later, outside the courtroom, Dr. Smith told John Milgrim of the *Times Herald Record* that Wendy was guilty, but of manslaughter, not murder. "My opinion is that the appropriate thing is for her to get the extreme emotional disturbance reduction."

James Evans, though, was another story.

"He is, without a doubt, very psychopathic. It is one of the cases I'm one hundred percent certain about. He is a killer."

Milgrim asked again about Wendy.

"She, in my opinion, is not a criminal," said the psychiatrist, restating the point of his testimony. "She's a young girl gone astray, that needs to be sort of retrained, if you will. James is different. James is not retrainable."

Wendy's comment about the Christmas presents—a ludicrous lie in light of the other testimony in the case—never made it to Milgrim's story.

Flaherty had one more witness to end the day with, a kind of topper to Smith: Clarence "Buzz" Gardner.

Wendy's father had stayed by her side all through the ordeal of her trial. If he had been a less than ideal father to her in her early years, perhaps he tried to atone somewhat by showing her the love and attention she had never had before.

But Flaherty didn't call him to the front of the room to give him a Father's Day card. What the lawyer wanted was a portrait of a man wracked by drug and alcohol problems, a father more absent than present. Miranda inadvertently helped out by provoking Buzz's anger during a brief cross-examination, but it was Flaherty who drove the main point home about Wendy's poor childhood.

"Is it fair to say you were never really a father to

Wendy?'' asked the attorney as he wrapped up his questioning.

"Yes," said Buzz Gardner.

He looked over at the round, childish face. There was so much to regret, so much to wish vainly had never happened. The courtroom was filled with demons, not a few of whom he had conjured up himself.

"I should be sitting where she is," said Buzz.

33

In her own defense

February 19, 1997

Wendy Gardner had wanted to tell her story for years now. She wanted everyone in the world to know what her grandmother had done to her. If they listened to her, if the jury heard her, then no one would condemn her.

Today she was going to get that chance. She gazed into the mirror as she fixed her hair, getting ready to begin the long journey to the courtroom. The clear eyes that gazed back weren't those of a murderer. The soft face belonged to a kid, not a killer.

Lisa Beth Older had spent considerable time preparing Wendy to testify, even staying at a motel near the detention center to facilitate the interviews. When Older called her witness to the stand Wednesday morning, she knew precisely what to expect.

Flaherty remained at the defense table, part of him hoping for the best, most of him stewing. He blamed Buzz for this, and Older. Wendy Gardner was starved for maternal love, and for some weird reason had found it in Older.

But damn. Even as the kid began talking, he could see her cold, distanced voice wasn't making a good impression on the jury.

Older asked about James, asked about her grandmother. Did she want her grandmother killed?

"I never literally meant I wanted my grandmother to die," she testified. "I loved her."

But, Gardner told the court, her grandmother used to slap her in the face and paddle her, tell her she was going to grow up just like her mother. She was a hard woman who meted out harsh punishments.

Flaherty kept a poker face, but it would have been hard to deny that the main part of his defense was being undermined by his own client. The tape was bad enough, but at least he had gotten Smith to cite Wendy as a "poor historian." The lawyer could explain the confession away as one more attempt by the girl to keep her psychological kidnapper on her side. But the more Wendy seemed to blame her grandmother, the more it detracted from James Evans as the villain of the story. Though Flaherty had drawn out instances of possible abuse with several witnesses, there was simply no way to effectively draw the grandmother's actions as bad enough to justify murder.

The tape Miranda had played presented the defense with serious problems, and as Gardner continued to testify, Older attempted to undermine the statements she had made to the police. The girl noted that she was only thirteen when the murder occurred; she thought things like that only happened in the movies.

What about James, Older asked.

"It's like there were two sides to him," Wendy answered. Many times he was nice, giving her gifts; they would go on walks and go bowling together. But he could suddenly become very vicious. "He grabbed and pushed me into a car and said he would rip my throat out if I tried to leave him," she testified.

In the audience, Dinah Evans bit her lip. She liked Wendy, despite everything, and she still thought there was a lot of good in the kid. But in her opinion, Wendy Gardner was lying. The more she talked, the deeper she went. Even Dinah could tell the jury didn't buy it.

Assistant District Attorney Miranda watched the jury as well, and bided his time.

Older's examination continued for about an hour. She topped it off by asking Wendy to make a statement.

Wendy looked at the jury. "I didn't want my grandmother to die. After all the things she did to me I still loved her. I love my sister. Even now, I still love my family."

The stoic voice suddenly broke. Wendy Gardner began to cry.

"I'm glad that you listened to me," she told the jury.

* * *

In the audience, one of Betty Gardner's sisters struggled to control a typhoon of anger and resentment as the girl finished.

The little actress, she thought to herself. *She ought to get an Academy Award for her lying.*

"You enjoyed the sex, didn't you?" Miranda demanded when it was his turn to examine her.

"Sometimes, yes."

Gardner tried to add that there were times she didn't. Miranda, fully in control, balancing his pose between thoughtful prosecutor and committed avenger of justice, continued on. He wasn't vicious. There was no need to be. Gardner was hanging herself. But he was relentless.

On the night of December 28, did she try to stop James from killing her grandmother?

"No, I didn't."

Why not?

Well, she was afraid, she was frightened, she thought she might be next. Or her sister.

"I didn't want to believe what was happening," Gardner told Miranda.

And later, she couldn't run?

She was scared.

Why had she helped James stuff the body in the trunk?

She was scared.

Why had she gone on a shopping spree, spending all that money her grandmother had had?

She was scared.

She couldn't call the police at any point? Couldn't run away? Couldn't turn him in?

She was scared.

"Who did you trust more: the police or James Evans?" Miranda demanded.

"I didn't trust anyone."

And her statement to the police? It was a lie?

"Yes."

But she wasn't lying now?

No, she was telling the truth.

"It is your fault that your grandmother is dead," said the prosecutor. "Isn't that correct?"

"If I wouldn't have said anything, I don't believe it would have happened."

Case made and underlined, Miranda sat down.

Jeremiah Flaherty called his own psychiatrist, John Lucas, that afternoon. Lucas's findings paralleled Kevin Smith's. When he had been diagramming his strategy, Flaherty thought that Lucas would provide a tidy restatement of the emotional disturbance plea. But, maybe because of the emotions unleashed by Gardner earlier that morning, the testimony seemed flat.

Lucas had talked to Wendy, her father, and two other people who knew her. He came away convinced that she had a tendency to distort reality and lose control in emotional situations. It was the combination of the two kids together that did in Betty Gardner, he felt. As he put it later outside court, James was the Velcro that matched Wendy's hooks.

The metaphor was too apt to help the defense very much.

Lucas reinforced many of the themes Smith had opened up, and also supplied information about Gardner's childhood. He noted that Buzz had told him Jann used cocaine and heroin while she was pregnant with the girl.

Flaherty also had Lucas make an important point: Wendy would appear emotionless on the stand because it was part of a defense mechanism. She naturally distanced herself from emotions. But he couldn't undo the damage she had done to herself. The psychiatrist as much as said the girl was not a murderer, that she had been manipulated by James, but anyone listening to his testimony now had to weigh that against Miranda's questions and Gardner's own admissions.

If she had been so afraid of James Evans, why hadn't she gone to the police? She'd had plenty of time and opportunity.

With no more witnesses to call, the defense rested.

34

Justice

The jurors listened intently as Judge Bruhn finished his summary of the legal grounds for emotional disturbance. Already this morning they had heard closing arguments from both sides, one calling for the lesser charge of manslaughter, one saying that nothing less than a verdict of murder would be acceptable.

The white-haired Jeremiah Flaherty had gone first. Carrying himself a bit like a boxer, with a city accent and gestures that jabbed the air, he had told the eight men and four women that the case "in a nutshell, is about force and seduction." The term, as most of them remembered, was a reference to something one of the psychiatrists had said. There had been no contesting the fact that Betty Gardner had died at the hands of James Evans. Flaherty wanted the jurors to believe that

Wendy Gardner had been manipulated into going along.

But the prosecutor had answered that Wendy Gardner had been the manipulator. Her relationship with James Evans had been part of it.

"She got what she wanted," Mike Miranda told them, pointing back at her. "The death of Mrs. Gardner."

He hadn't been quite as feisty as Flaherty, nor as well-dressed, but Miranda came off like a regular guy, somebody like them, somebody interested in justice.

The prosecutor admitted that Wendy Gardner had had a less than ideal life, but the house on Appletree Drive had been far from the worst place to grow up. "I daresay twenty-five percent of you have had a worse life than these kids," Miranda had said.

The victim had worked all her life to give this poor kid love. Did she deserve to be repaid with murder?

Now it was up to them. Judge Bruhn concluded his explanation of the legal issues involved in the trial and sent them out to debate a verdict.

As soon as they reached the jury room, two of the jurors said they had already decided Wendy Gardner was guilty of murder.

But some of the others weren't sure. Did extreme emotional disturbance mean that any emotional factor was an argument for manslaughter? How much would it take for the lesser charge?

The jurors debated the issue, then asked to see Wendy's diary and other pieces of physical evidence. They asked for Kathy Gardner's and Dr. Smith's testimony read back to them.

They also asked for Wendy Gardner's testimony.

Lucas, cut up by Miranda on cross-examination, wasn't given much credibility. The jurors felt that he had merely repeated what Wendy told him. Since she hadn't convinced them, they weren't buying his interpretation.

But Smith seemed more potent. He'd admitted that Wendy was "a poor historian," implying that she couldn't be taken at face value. Even with that, he had been convinced she should get the lesser charge.

The deliberations stretched toward nine o'clock before the twelve adjourned for the night. By then, there seemed to be a ten-two split among the jurors in favor of the more severe charge of murder, with the two holdouts arguing that Wendy's age ought to be a primary factor in considering the verdict.

Outside the courthouse, the press was keeping a vigil, waiting for the verdict to come in. The trial of the youngest murderers ever in Ulster County had affected the reporters in many different ways. They felt that something special was going on, something more than just a news story.

They wanted to be part of it. Cynthia Werthamer was thinking about writing a screenplay; John Milgrim was toying with the idea of writing a book.

The impulse was not terribly different than what James Evans had felt, listening to his rap tapes, or Wendy Gardner, watching *Snapdragon*. It was as if the case could vault them from the everyday drudgery of court proceedings and police arrests to some mythic kingdom of significance, a world only partly realized in reality. In America, you're only real if you're in a movie or a song.

                          *   *   *

The jury resumed deliberations the next day shortly
after 9 A.M. Almost immediately, the jurors asked the
judge to reread the explanation of the law pertaining
to extreme emotional disturbance.

Whether it was the judge's explanation or the night
off to think, the opinions against Wendy Gardner had
hardened. Where there had been confusion the night
before, now the majority were strongly convinced that
the girl was a cold-blooded murderer. Even the two
jurors who had been thinking about how young she was
were swayed by the others' arguments, finally disre-
garding her age and agreeing that there wasn't enough
evidence of abuse to justify the extreme emotional
defense. They weren't happy about it but they agreed.
One later told a reporter he cried after the decision.

At 11:25 A.M., the jury foreman notified the judge that
a verdict had been reached. Gardner, her attorneys,
and the assistant district attorney were assembled; the
press was notified. The twelve men and women were
led back into the courtroom. A few gazed at the girl
sitting at the table, a few didn't.

Outside, clouds had gathered and the air was cold
and raw as winter lingered. Work in the courthouse
had been temporarily halted. Thick coats rustled in the
audience as a few last-minute stragglers settled into their
chairs. Finally, everyone was still.

The judge looked to the foreman. Had the jury
reached a verdict?

They had.

Guilty. Murder in the second degree.

One by one, the jurors were polled.

Guilty, murder in the second degree, each repeated.

Wendy Gardner began to cry.

As the jurors were led out of the room, Wendy rose slowly and held her hands out in front of her for the handcuffs. She seemed stunned by the verdict. Tears flowing, she walked quietly with the guards as she was led to a holding area to wait for transport back to jail. When the doors closed on her, her soft sobs turned to loud, mournful wails.

Outside, one of the jurors passed a note to a reporter.

"This kind of behavior in our society won't be tolerated. Justice has been served."

VIII

Epilogue

35

"Just shut up"

April 9, 1997

Riding up the elevator of the old courthouse, Betty Gardner's relatives discussed recipes and Florida, a trip to Ireland—everything but the murder. They had lived with it now for more than two years. Tragedies like this never really ended, but the sentencing today would provide some sense of closure, at least.

The elevator stopped on the second floor and the women got out, making their way slowly toward the courtroom. They took their place in the middle of the three long, makeshift rows of metal chairs. The jury box was already filled with media people and reporters.

The building was still being renovated. Despite the fact that the calendar said spring, the temperature outside remained below freezing and records were being set. Just the other week there had been a bona fide blizzard, shutting the whole county down. Everyone in the courtroom still wore winter clothing.

The time set for the sentencing hearing came and went. The defendant had not yet arrived at the courthouse. Judge Bruhn held a brief conference with the journalists, making sure that the court's rules stipulating the location and use of cameras would be followed

People milled around. One of Betty Gardner's sisters talked about seeing Wendy on a television show.

"She needs help, that girl."

Someone asked about a special family recipe.

Sometime after 10:30, Court Clerk Charles Roach entered the back of the room. "Judge in the court," he said, walking forward briskly. "All rise."

Bruhn, Hush Puppies peeking out from beneath his long flowing robes, followed through the crowd. While he had chosen to use the back door because of the construction, it made him appear the very embodiment of democratic justice, a robed figure emerging from the crowd to render his sentence. The short walk seemed to transform him from an easygoing, mild-mannered lawyer to a kind but firm conscience of the people. His voice deepened, and physically he became considerably more deliberate.

Wendy Gardner came next. Her steps were short, choked by the manacles that bound her feet together. She wore a plush brown velvet dress cut mid-thigh. In her fingers were blue rosary beads. Scared and frightened, she came to hear her sentence like a persecuted mouse. Jeremiah Flaherty towered above her at the defense table.

The cameras clicked away.

Mike Miranda waited at the defense table. His boss had said immediately after the trial that he would not ask for the maximum; all the newspapers had carried the story. While not letting the teenagers off the hook, Kavanagh's sense of justice told him the parents bore a great deal of the blame for the murder. He agreed with Buzz Gardner when he'd said he ought to be the one on trial. Kavanagh even admitted, much later, that he wouldn't have been heartbroken to see the jury convict Wendy of manslaughter instead of murder.

But somewhere along the way, the politically sensitive district attorney had changed his mind about asking the judge to go easy, and Miranda showed no quarter now, even as he spoke in somewhat generous tones about the fine job the jury, the judge, and even defense attorney Jerry Flaherty had done.

The assistant district attorney felt that some part of what Dr. Smith and Dr. Lucas had told the jury about Wendy—not a hundred percent, maybe not even fifty percent, but a significant part nonetheless—was probably true. Something troubled that kid; she'd definitely been messed up. He also thought she was pretty smart and might—would—rehabilitate herself.

But he wasn't going to admit it today. That wasn't his job. His job was justice, and that required putting Wendy Gardner away for as long as possible.

The assistant DA read a letter from Betty Gardner's sister June calling James Evans a puppet in Wendy's hands. "The tragic part in all of this is Elizabeth Gardner only wanted the best for Wendy," June wrote. "She loved her and wanted her to grow up to be a lady."

June wanted the maximum sentence, nine years to life.

Betty's relatives nodded as the assistant district attorney asked Bruhn to forget how young Wendy was. "Take into account that Elizabeth Gardner is dead," he urged. "And why?"

Why, Miranda repeated. Why was Betty Gardner killed?

Wendy Gardner should be made to answer that question before she was ever granted parole. And she shouldn't get the chance to do that for at least nine years, the maximum sentence allowed by law.

Now it was Flaherty's turn. He fixed a button on his double-breasted tan suit as he rose. Somehow he had picked up Wendy's rosary beads, and unconsciously played with them as he spoke to the judge. "She is a girl," he told Bruhn, recalling Smith's testimony. Then he echoed Lucas's line about the "force of seduction."

"This kid was wide open," Flaherty said, as if he were retrying the case. "This is the same sort of situation with terrorists and hostages."

By now, Betty Gardner's relatives were beginning to grow restless. One of her sisters adjusted the collar on her coat, brushing off imaginary lint.

"This kid will never know why this occurred," Flaherty said, flashing some of the fire he had shown during the trial. "If we think that she will have an answer, we're kidding ourselves. The real story in this case is, two teenagers committed a senseless act."

Then the lawyer pulled out a photocopy of some notes that had been found in the house after it was sold. They seem to have been made in connection with the PINS petition, though Flaherty didn't mention that.

" 'This guy has her controlled,' " he quoted. " 'He would call her up just to say he had her controlled.' "

Wendy began to sob as Flaherty continued. In the brief, bare notes, Betty said that she loved Wendy but didn't know how to reach her.

"We're not saying the grandmother was an ogre," said Flaherty, nonetheless hinting that Betty had gone overboard in disciplining the girl. No one was there to help her, he continued. No one—not even her other relatives.

"We do this too much in society. We just all look the other way, all of us. We all come here today to see a fifteen-year-old kid get sentenced, but when she was six or seven, there was no one there."

"I wish he'd just shut up," hissed one of Betty's sisters.

When Flaherty finished, Wendy Gardner rose and her handcuffs were removed. Then she began speaking to the judge, her voice barely audible over the ventilation system.

"Every morning when I wake up I look at myself in the mirror. I can't tell myself I'm the murderer."

Her voice cracked.

"I never really thought any of this would happen," she added, clutching the holy beads. "I just want to say I'm sorry."

It was not Judge Bruhn's custom to prepare an elaborate speech, and he did not break that custom this morning. His comments were succinct, delivered in a weighty tone that seemed to come as much from the bench as his own mouth.

He had presided over both cases, and he felt that it had taken both teenagers to commit the murder. Remove one or the other from the equation, and Betty Gardner would still be alive.

"It frightens me, the comment that Mr. Flaherty

made, that you don't know why it happened,'' said the judge. "I don't want you to go back into society without knowing why.''

Wendy, standing next to her lawyer with hands clasped around the dangling rosary beads, looked at the floor. Flaherty knotted his fingers a little tighter, looking every bit as contrite and humble as his client.

New York's sentencing guidelines did not leave the judge with a large amount of leeway in deciding the sentence. The least he could sentence her to was five years to life; the most, nine years to life. He had, however, carefully considered the possibilities, and so arrived at a highly precise, if somewhat unusual, sentence: seven years, ten months, twenty-five days minimum. Maximum, life.

By his calculations, taking into account time served, the sentence meant that the earliest Wendy Gardner could be considered for parole was her twenty-first birthday.

It was still a long way off.

36

A last word

Spring 1997

The weather that spring eventually warmed. The memory of the case lingered for some, faded for others.

I had followed it from a distance, mostly by reading newspaper reports, until Wendy's trial. Like everyone else, the question of "Why?" got to me. I decided to write this book as a way of finding out.

I began talking to people who might have at least some part of the answer. I read Wendy's diary, which had never made it into the newspapers. I ran into what seemed a paranoid wall of silence at the school district, where the convenient excuse of confidentiality had kept anyone from asking in public what district personnel might have done differently to help a student so clearly in trouble. I learned about Wendy's symptoms of cutting, an obvious sign of mental distress but unremarked by anyone, including the psychiatrists. And I discovered what the "Snapdraggon" references in her diary were all about, something not even the assistant DA had been able to find out.

I also encountered family members who absolutely refused to comment. And I had one conversation with Buzz Gardner that went, roughly, like this:

> Buzz: How much money do you got?
> Me: Me? Not very much.
> Buzz: Then I'm not talking to you.

A few people thought I was a ghoul or worse, I'm sure. But most were helpful and sincerely interested in what I might find out. They, too, wanted to know why the murder had occurred. Why had a thirteen-year-old girl killed her own grandmother?

It was clear to me from the beginning that both James and Wendy were guilty of killing Betty Gardner. As I delved into the case, it also became clear that there was so much blame that parceling out who deserved which portion, who was guiltier than whom, was an exercise in trivia.

As I continued to talk to people, it seemed to me that Mike Miranda's question at the sentencing, "Why did this happen?" had been adequately answered. The problem was, and remains, that it didn't come together in a neat, monosyllabic sentence; it didn't happen in an isolated moment. It wasn't just sex, or money, or a senseless act. It wasn't just retribution, or just anger. It wasn't something a psychiatric expert could put into a quotable sentence for a newspaper. Our culture's preoccupation with violence, the society's emphasis on gangster images, the glorification of death—all had a part.

So did the custody battle that twisted James and taught him to defy authority. So did something in James' own makeup. So did Wendy's preoccupation with sex, and her desperate need to feel loved. So did her childhood and estrangement. So did the emotional abuse she felt she received from so many sources, including her grandmother.

The problem was, it was difficult to face it all. Because if we admitted why the murder had happened, if we acknowledged the many things that had contributed, we would be admitting our own culpability.

I didn't get that until one Saturday afternoon when I started talking about the case with one of the state troopers who had played a critical role in the investigation. Somehow, we got philosophical; I said something along the lines that a person has to take responsibility for his or her own actions.

"What about society?" he asked. What about the institutions that are supposed to help out—that were supposed to do something, and ended up making things worse.

Didn't they bear part of the guilt?

A few months later, I took a trip to Saugerties, N.Y., one of many I made in the course of researching this book. But I wasn't going to talk to anyone, not out loud anyway. I went to stop at Betty Gardner's grave, and to light a candle at her church.

It was a bright, sunny day; I had the cemetery to myself. I kept thinking about how complicated life can get, how here was a woman who went out of her way to do the right thing and got paid back with murder— how she had carried some seeds of the tragedy within herself, like a Greek hero in an ancient play trying to stand up to the gods despite a fatal flaw.

An hour later, I walked up the hillside of St. Mary of the Snow, passing the markers erected to the memories of simple men and women who had built Saugerties and America. Betty had been particularly proud of her Irish forebears; I couldn't help but think of my own Irish-American grandmother, who'd sacrificed everything for her kids, raising them in Washington Heights during and after the Depression and war.

Inside the church, I went to the side altar, hoping to light a candle. When I had first started working on the book, I had promised myself I would light one for Betty Gardner; she was a devout Catholic, and any old-line true believer knows that time in purgatory can be shortened by the prayers of those on earth.

As I walked up the aisle after mass, however, I realized she wasn't the one who needed prayer; her eternal soul had already found its place in the afterlife. It is those who were left behind—all of us, not simply the family or friends—who need to find a way to cope with our bloody inheritance, who must find strength to not just do the right thing for those we know, but for those we don't know. As Flaherty had said at the sentencing, all too often we turn away at moments when it might yet make a difference.

I walked to the front with determination, the prayer forming on my lips, my hand reaching into my pocket for an offering. But I found all the candles already burning.

Author's note

This book is based on extensive interviews, observation, and reporting by the author, court documents, records and transcripts, published reports, and other materials. All quoted dialogue comes directly from transcripts, interviews or other documented sources. Thoughts and paraphrases, not inside quotes, are likewise based on my research.

In many cases, I have had to interpret between conflicting versions of a particular event, sometimes from the same source. I have tried to include credible alternative versions where appropriate.

The transcripts of the trials were not prepared in time for the completion of this book. My accounts of the court proceedings are based on trial notes, published reports, eyewitness accounts, interviews with the participants and personal observation.

Too many people cooperated with me for me to thank

each one personally here. Many, though far from all, are identified by name in the text. A special thanks also goes to the many clerks and other "ordinary people" not connected with the case, but who helped in a hundred different ways, directly and indirectly. There were people like Rose Simoneau, for example, a receptionist in the Ulster County District Attorney's Office who spoke with me on an almost daily basis for several months, helping me track down and arrange appointments with different members of the DA's office. And then there were others like Charles "Chuck" Roach, a tireless county court clerk who braved dust and cobwebs to help locate materials relevant to the case. Finally, while the New York State Troopers' Bureau of Criminal Investigation is well represented in the book, space and the narrative form did not permit all of the investigators and troopers who worked on the case to be mentioned. The BCI's Forensics Identification unit in particular played an important but unsung role in closing this case, like so many others; because of the circumstances, and the unit's high degree of competence, that role was utterly devoid of drama. But I would be remiss if I didn't mention the unit's cooperation, especially in the person of Senior Investigator Donald B. Markert, in the preparation of this book.

One person who held the key to so much that remains a mystery—but who naturally could not be interviewed—was the murder victim, Betty Gardner. Catholics believe that if a person dies while in a state of grace, her soul will make its way to eternal peace. Hopefully, hers is on its way.

HORRIFYING TRUE CRIME
FROM PINNACLE BOOKS

Body Count
by Burl Barer   0-7860-1405-9   **$6.50**US/**$8.50**CAN

The Babyface Killer
by Jon Bellini   0-7860-1202-1   **$6.50**US/**$8.50**CAN

Love Me to Death
by Steve Jackson   0-7860-1458-X   **$6.50**US/**$8.50**CAN

The Boston Stranglers
by Susan Kelly   0-7860-1466-0   **$6.50**US/**$8.50**CAN

Body Double
by Don Lasseter   0-7860-1474-1   **$6.50**US/**$8.50**CAN

The Killers Next Door
by Joel Norris   0-7860-1502-0   **$6.50**US/**$8.50**CAN

Available Wherever Books Are Sold!

Visit our website at **www.kensingtonbooks.com**.

MORE MUST-READ TRUE CRIME FROM PINNACLE

Slow Death   0-7860-1199-8   **$6.50**US/**$8.99**CAN
By James Fielder

Fatal Journey   0-7860-1578-0   **$6.50**US/**$8.99**CAN
By Jack Gieck

Partners in Evil   0-7860-1521-7   **$6.50**US/**$8.99**CAN
By Steve Jackson

Dead and Buried   0-7860-1517-9   **$6.50**US/**$8.99**CAN
By Corey Mitchell

Perfect Poison   0-7860-1550-0   **$6.50**US/**$8.99**CAN
By M. William Phelps

Family Blood   0-7860-1551-9   **$6.50**US/**$8.99**CAN
By Lyn Riddle

Available Wherever Books Are Sold!

Visit our website at **www.kensingtonbooks.com**.

More Thrilling Suspense From
T.J. MacGregor

The Hanged Man	0-7860-0646-3	$5.99US/$7.50CAN
The Seventh Sense	0-7860-1083-5	$6.99US/$8.99CAN
Vanished	0-7860-1162-9	$6.99US/$8.99CAN
The Other Extreme	0-7860-1322-2	$6.99US/$8.99CAN
Out of Sight	0-7860-1323-0	$6.99US/$9.99CAN
Black Water	0-7860-1557-8	$6.99US/$9.99CAN

Available Wherever Books Are Sold!

Visit our website at **www.kensingtonbooks.com**

Feel the Seduction Of
Pinnacle Horror